Intensive Kids – Intensive Interventions

Designing School Programs for Behaviorally Disordered Children & Youth

Kevin I. Coats, Ph.D., NCSP

Universal Publishers
Boca Raton, Florida
USA • 2006

Intensive Kids – Intensive Interventions:
Designing School Programs for Behaviorally Disordered
Children & Youth

Copyright © 2006 Kevin I. Coats

Universal Publishers
Boca Raton, Florida • USA
2004

ISBN: 1-58112- 916-5

www.universal-publishers.com

This book is dedicated to the children at the
Broad Street Teaching and Learning Center who have
allowed me to be a part of their lives.

TABLE OF CONTENTS

ACKNOWLEDGEMENTS

I wish to thank many people who have helped make this book possible. First, to my wife, Barbara, for her never-ending support and encouragement throughout this entire process. To my sons, Aaron and Matt, who are the source of so much joy and energy in my life.

Next, my gratitude to teachers and mentors who have been so influential in the role they have played in helping shape my career. As a professor at McGill University, Dr. Virginia Douglas first inspired me to work with disabled children and encouraged me to become a school psychologist. I thank her for guiding me in that direction. Drs. William Reynolds, William Gardner, Dorothy Loeb and Beverly Bliss, my professors at the University of Wisconsin-Madison, taught me important lessons about working with children and families, always believed in me and gave me the tools to get started in my career as a helping professional. Their knowledge and support were invaluable. I also wish to thank Les Hynum, my colleague and friend, with the Milton, Wisconsin area schools who guided me when I first began working as a psychologist in the schools. His respect and understanding of children along with his unending sense of humor, served as a wonderful example on how a school psychologist should practice.

A special thanks goes to the Washington-Saratoga-Warren-Hamilton-Essex Counties' Board of Cooperative Educational Services in Hudson Falls, New York for granting me the time to research and write this book. Their support of school psychological services and professional development activities in general, serves as a positive example for all school agencies to follow. I am also grateful to Rebekah Galy, editor with Universal Publishers, who initially reviewed my manuscript and made it possible to produce this book.

And finally, to all the educators, counselors and therapists I have been privileged to meet, thank you for your insights about teaching, learning and promoting mental health in children. Your ideas about what it takes to help children with challenging behaviors can be found on each page of this book.

PREFACE

Schools want to improve their programs and services for all students, including those who arrive at the school door with serious behavioral and mental health problems. Indeed, recent federal mandates described in the Amendments to the Individuals with Disabilities Act (IDEA) specify that when the need directly affects learning, the school must meet the challenge. Unfortunately, most school administrators, teachers, school psychologists and other educators recognize that serving children with serious emotional and behavioral disorders (SED) is a daunting task and they have few resources to help guide them. All too often schools fall short in their efforts to establish comprehensive, multifaceted and cohesive approaches to serving this population. In response, *Intensive Kids – Intensive Interventions* is written as a practical guide to help school officials plan and implement alternative programs that can ensure that even the most troubled students have an equal opportunity to succeed at school.

What should happen to an 11 year old boy who brings a weapon to school? How can a school best respond to a middle school student who has a chronic record of school violence toward teachers and peers? Children with serious emotional disturbance (SED) present significant challenges for schools from at least two perspectives.

First, is the understanding that behavioral and mental health problems can dramatically interfere with learning and other areas of functioning. There is little doubt that this can lead to negative life outcomes for the individual and result in serious costs to society. Second, and in light of recent school shooting tragedies across the country, the public is also demanding that schools provide a safe and responsive learning environment for all students.

Consequently, effective alternative programs are needed to balance the right of all children to a safe school with the right of children with intensive behavioral disorders to an appropriate education. To address both of these critical needs, schools are under intense pressure to develop effective programs for troubled children and youth.

Unfortunately, alternative programs for troubled students have often been nothing more than dumping grounds for kids who could not fit into regular education. Historically, alternative program policies and procedures have in many instances relied on highly punitive, coercive approaches to student discipline and have only created further alienation and despair for students. Clearly, this need not nor should it be the case.

Over the past 20 years the literature on behavior management and empirically validated interventions for troubled children has grown tremendously. Unfortunately, the busy school administrator or practitioner has little time to access this information or sift through an ever-growing body of journals and books on this subject in order to create productive learning environments for troubled kids. Given the practical realities of life in schools, I have attempted to write a book for school leaders and school-based mental health providers that can serve as a resource guide that combines much of this information in one text. Specifically, the book addresses a number of key questions. What do effective programs look like? What specific strategies can schools use? What current resources exist that provide direct support for program development efforts? How will you know that your program is effective?

It is my sincere hope that this text will offer useful information that can assist the reader in finding answers to these and other questions in a very straightforward and practical format. With this in mind, the book serves as a no nonsense guide for developing and implementing high-quality school-based programs for students with intensive behavioral and mental health needs.

Most of the material for this book comes from my 28 years of experience as a psychologist in the schools and, in particular, from my work at the Broad Street Teaching and Learning Center - a therapeutic day school for seriously emotionally and behaviorally disordered children located in upstate New York. While at the Broad Street Center, I have had the good fortune of developing, using and testing many of the policies and procedures that are included within the book. In 1998, our program was identified as an exemplary model for serving SED children in a publication entitled, *Exemplary Mental Health Programs: School Psychologists as Mental Health Service*

Providers (Nastasi, Vargas and Bernstein, 1998). In addition, other schools in New York have successfully adopted at least portions of the ideas contained in this book as they have gone forward to develop new programs for SED children in their own districts. By way of disclaimer, I should state that a bulk of the information contained in this text comes from other authors who have written extensively on topics pertaining to schools and the needs of SED students. With this in mind, I would encourage the reader to explore many of the ideas and concepts that are presented in the book in further depth.

Kevin I. Coats, Ph.D., NCSP

CHAPTER 1

THE NEED FOR PROGRAMS AND SERVICES

INTRODUCTION

Children with severe emotional and behavioral disorders have, for many years, provided a daunting challenge for educators within traditional school settings. Teachers and administrators have always struggled in knowing what to do with students who exhibit chronic behavior problems, particularly those who display more serious misconduct (Crews & Counts, 1997). This is especially troubling when one considers the sobering fact that challenging behaviors can consume up to 80% of a teacher's instructional time (Sugai & Horner, 1994). Behavior problems disrupt not only the teaching and learning process but may also result in school exclusion for the child that engages in severe forms of disruptive or dangerous behavior.

As our society changes, it is quite probable that schools will be seeing more children who are regularly disruptive over extended periods of time resulting in negative consequences for themselves, teachers, peers and the community. Many of these children who walk through our school doors come from families who are in significant turmoil themselves. In addition to intraindividual factors (psychological, prematurity and other health-related, social-cognitive), the research is quite clear in terms of what familial factors relate to childhood aggression, mental health problems and disruptive behavior in the classroom. Many of these children come from homes that have a higher than average divorce rate, alcohol and drug use, physical and sexual abuse, poverty, poor supervision and monitoring of behavior, inconsistent discipline, low parental expectations, caregiver mental health problems and an unhealthy diet of exposure to violent behavior in the media and video games (Halpern, 1990; Minke & Bear, 2000). Unfortunately, a host of other factors including negative peer affiliation and classroom/school factors (e.g., unfair rules and disciplinary practices, class size, school climate, teacher skills and expectations, availability of resources) also contribute to student aggression.

Awareness and understanding of these factors is important particularly when trying to determine whether to "fix" the child or "fix" the system. Professionals in the mental health field have commonly looked at children manifesting behavioral, emotional and learning problems as having some type of internal pathology. While this can often be helpful in facilitating treatment decisions, it can also result in blaming the victim which places the focus on the individual rather than system weaknesses that are causing the problem. Most practitioners, however, who use diagnostic labels would also recognize that problems in human behavior result from the reciprocal interplay between person and his or her environment (Bandura, 1978).

Adelman and Taylor (1993) provide a transactional view of the primary locus of cause related to behavioral, emotional and learning problems. Problems are placed along a continuum that ranges from those caused by environmental factors (Type I problems) at one extreme to those caused by internal factors (Type III problems) at the other extreme. Type II factors involve problems caused equally by environment and person. For example, a child with early onset Bi-Polar Disorder or severe Attention Deficit Hyperactivity Disorder would fit the Type III category since the behavioral problems are a result of pathology within the individual. The behavior problems of a child who grows up in a hostile home environment would be viewed as a result of factors outside the person (i.e., Type I problems). While this continuum may oversimplify the enormous complexities in understanding the relationship between psychopathology and environmental-social problems, it does provide a useful model for understanding cause and correction. Specifically, it reduces the tendency to "blame the victim" (Ryan, 1971) and highlights the notion that problems may be reduced or alleviated by improving the way the environment accommodates individual differences in students.

THE SCOPE OF THE PROBLEM

What do we actually know about the extent to which children are in need of social-emotional, behavioral or other mental health support? According to recent studies (Sprague,

Sugai & Walker, 1998; Todd, Horner, Sugai & Colvin, 1999), in the typical school, almost one quarter of students exhibit problematic behaviors in some degree and an estimated three to seven percent engage in behaviors serious enough to require specialized intervention. There is also evidence to suggest that the problem is not only increasing but more widespread than most people might imagine. In a recent study by the Metropolitan Life Insurance Company (1999), incidents of seriously disruptive and violent behavior were found equally likely to happen in both urban and rural settings as well as across elementary, middle and high school campuses.

According to a recent Surgeon General's Report on Mental Health (1999) and a companion follow-up report entitled, *Report of the Surgeon General's Conference on Children's Mental Health: A National Action Agenda (2001)*, our nation is facing a crisis in mental healthcare for infants, children and adolescents. Estimates identify approximately 20% of children and youth under age 18 who have mental health disorders. In any given year, however, only one in five children receive specialty mental health services and unmet needs for services remain about as high now as they were 20 years ago (Burns, et al., 1995). Prevalence estimates of mental health disorders in youth reported by Costello et al. (1996) ranged from 17.6 to 22% and 16% in another study (Roberts, 1998). When considering that one out of five children experience problems that may directly affect their chances of success in life, there is clearly a pressing need to focus efforts on prevention, early intervention and treatment for complex cases. Certainly, the societal cost is enormous in terms of both human and fiscal waste.

A number of expert contributors to the Surgeon General's Report (2001) highlighted the need to train school professionals to recognize early symptoms of emotional and behavioral disorders and to improve services in schools utilizing effective, research-based programs and interventions for school-wide, targeted (at-risk) and intensive need populations. Without greater attention devoted to these objectives, it is likely that we will continue to see many children and youth fall through the cracks. As many professionals in the juvenile justice system are well aware, too often youth who are not identified as having mental health problems and fail to receive services or at least adequate services, end up in jail.   As a practitioner in the schools over the past 28 years, I know too well that children with mental health problems are also at much greater risk of dropping out of school, joining the ranks of the juvenile justice and child welfare systems and not being fully functional members of society in adulthood.

Studies looking at youth violence are also raising concern among school professionals and the public with results showing dramatic increases in violence rates during the past fifteen years. In a report published by the Centers for Disease Control National Center for Injury Control and Prevention (1996), homicide was found to become the second leading cause of death for youth ages 15 to 24 and the leading cause of death for black Americans in this same age group.   Annual arrest rates for weapons carrying charges for youth under 18 years of age increased at an alarming rate of 104%.

Interestingly and despite the media attention given to the deadly shooting tragedies that have occurred in recent years, a very small proportion of the violence reported for children actually takes place in school.   According to various national reports (Chandler, Chapman, Rand & Taylor, 1998; Heaviside, Rowand, Williams & Farris, 1998), less than one percent of homicides and suicides among children between 1992 and 1994 occurred in school.   However, a more disturbing statistic cited in a recent National Center for Educational Statistics Report, Violence and Discipline Problems in U. S. School: 1996-1997 (Heaviside et. al., 1998), was a strong relationship found between low level school disruption and more serious school violence.   In those schools that reported at least one serious discipline issue, 28% also reported at least one serious crime;   this compared with only 3% of schools with minor discipline problems that reported the existence of crime.   A study of three rural school districts (Peterson, Beekley, Speaker & Pietrzak, 1996) found that over half of the teachers and administrators believed school violence was increasing at the middle and high school levels.   Rather than the more extreme types of violence – weapons carrying, gang involvement, drug use – problems that were seen as increasing involved such behaviors as verbal threats and intimidation, rude behavior, sexual harassment, and pushing and shoving. What these findings would clearly suggest is that schools do need to pay close attention to school climate factors and disciplinary practices in order to reduce the risk that there may be more serious or violent acts.

KEY ISSUES IN THE DEBATE OVER WHAT TO DO WITH DISRUPTIVE STUDENTS

Zero Tolerance

Unfortunately, and in large part due to the school shooting tragedies across our nation in recent years, many school authorities have instituted "zero tolerance" policies that have been designed to keep schools safe yet have also resulted in the denial of educational opportunities for troubled students. Zero tolerance refers to policies that "punish all offenses severely, no matter how minor" (Skiba & Peterson, 1999, p. 373). Punishment typically involves some form of punishment such as in-school suspension, placement in an alternative program, exclusion or automatic school expulsion, with the latter causing perhaps the most controversy (Bear, Quinn & Burkholder, 2001). School suspension practices have not only been on the rise since the late 1970's but are also the number one choice used by schools to deal with severe behavior problems (Heaviside et al., 1998; McDonnell & Barren, 1994).

As a vehicle for responding to the increasing tide of school violence in the early 1990's, most states had begun instituting the policy of mandated expulsion for drugs, fighting and weapons possession. The signing into law of the Gun-Free Schools Act of 1994 helped make this a national policy by mandating a one-year expulsion for possession of a firearm. Subsequent amendments have broadened the language of the bill to include any object that might be considered a weapon. Although there is currently no federal mandate of automatic suspension for drug-related offenses, or other disruptive behaviors, the policy of zero tolerance has been increasingly applied to such behaviors as minor fighting, unauthorized use of pagers, possession of a fingernail file, sexual harassment (Skiba & Peterson, 1999), attendance problems (Morgan-D'Atrio, Northrup, LaFleur & Spera, 1996), and general classroom disruption (Imich, 1994; Morgan-D'Atrio et al., 1996). As a result, controversy over the practice of issuing severe punishments for relatively minor infractions has also grown, creating divided communities. Proponents of zero tolerance argue that we must send a clear message and "get serious" about discipline in order to stem the tide of school violence. Opponents caution that such policies serve only to teach students that schools are unjust systems and how to avoid or subvert rules and policies (Skiba, 2000).

No one would argue against the fact that such policies were initially crafted to help keep our schools safe and are appropriate as a means of responding to the most serious acts of violence (e.g., weapons, illicit drugs, vandalism, teacher assault). At the same time, they create outcomes that are probably reinforcing to administrators and teachers. However, others have clearly articulated the problems that surround overuse of out-of-school suspensions and expulsion. In fact, the research over the past 10 years has produced very limited evidence to support such widespread use (Mayer, 1995).

In their search for answers, investigators have raised two central questions. To what extent do such strategies work in changing student behavior and guaranteeing school safety? Do the positive benefits outweigh the potential negative side effects of school expulsion or suspension? Comprehensive reviews by Sciba (2000) and Heaviside et al. (1998) of the efficacy of school security measures (e.g., metal detectors, locker search, school uniforms, security personnel, surveillance cameras) as a component of zero tolerance practices were conducted. In these reviews, few empirical studies were found and there was little evidence other than school leader testimonials that zero tolerance improved school behavior or safety. In a National Center on Education Statistics study of school violence (Heaviside et al., 1998) and an extensive analysis of national data- bases conducted by Mayer & Leone (1999), school security measures – whether person or technology-based –were associated with increased reports of school violence and higher student fear of violence. In contrast, student awareness and enforcement of school rules were associated with decreased reports of school violence. The research on school uniforms is somewhat more positive in terms of the potential effect on school climate and teacher perceptions of school safety (Behling, 1994; Murray, 1997) although other studies have found that students do not perceive that uniforms have any positive influence on school safety (Sher, 1996; Stanley, 1996).

Although no known studies have been conducted that have examined the direct effects of school suspension on student behavior or school safety, other data would suggest that suspension is ineffective for those who are most likely to be targeted for disciplinary action. For example, researchers have reported that up to 40% of school suspensions are issued to repeat offenders (Bowditch, 1993; Costenbader & Markson, 1994) and that suspension is often a predictor of further suspension (Tobin, Sugai & Colvin, 1996). As one might imagine, repeated suspension is also linked to higher school dropout rates (Bowditch, 1993). It has been argued that repeated suspension for disruptive or at-risk students may actually contribute to an increase rather than decrease in problematic behaviors (Evans, 2002). At the very least, studies would suggest that, for some of our most troubled youth, their behavior does not improve as a result of suspension. Because these students are out of school they are, in fact, more likely to be at risk for a variety of negative outcomes including delinquency, substance abuse, unemployment and social maladjustment (Jenkins, 1997; Rossi, 1994).

While suspension definitely removes unwanted students from school, it may not occur without other unintended consequences. Various researchers (Gottfredson , 1989; Shores, Gunter & Jack, 1993) have found that more punitive and confrontational disciplinary strategies played a major role in escalating student misbehavior because students viewed such tactics as a "challenge" to which they must counter-react. Others (Hyman & Perone, 1998) have reported increases in anger and aggression among students who have been subjected to more intrusive security practices (e.g., undercover agents, personal searches). Certainly, the literature on punishment is very clear with respect to unintended consequences. Punishment does not result in learning of new skills. Rather, it is more likely to result in counter-aggression, escape/avoidance, habituation to even greater negative consequences and negative reinforcement of the punishing agent (Algozzine, Schmid & Mercer, 1981; Axelrod & Apsche, 1983; Skinner, 1953).

In summary, zero tolerance practices have raised a number of concerns for educators, parents and the public. There is a definite need for school officials to take strong actions that will deter violence and send a clear message that certain behaviors will not be tolerated. On the other hand, given the pressure on schools to do something, there is also the risk that many students will receive less than fair, equitable or reasonable treatment. As Skiba pointed out in his report entitled, *Zero Tolerance, Zero Evidence: An Analysis of School Disciplinary Practice* (Skiba, 2000), it is not that the goals of zero tolerance are in question but the methods of its implementation that lead to concern. What the literature on zero tolerance does suggest is that suspension has little to do with improved school behavior and safety and that alternative interventions to address discipline problems need to be promoted in our schools.

Inclusion

The debate over exactly where children with severe emotional and behavioral disabilities should be educated has never been fully resolved. This is probably due in large part to language put forth in IDEA that states that children with disabilities should be educated in the "least restrictive environment" and, to the maximum extent possible, with children who are nondisabled (34 CFR 300.550 (b) 1). However, sections of IDEA also state that schools should have a "continuum of alternative placements" available to meet the individual needs of students with disabilities (34CFR 300.551 (a).

On one side of the debate are proponents of full inclusion who believe that *all* students with disabilities should be educated with their nondisabled peers in regular settings. Supporting arguments typically cite the influence of teacher expectations and access to the full curriculum, the problem with "labeling" of students, student self-esteem, and association with prosocial peers. Critics argue that children with intensive mental health and behavioral needs require significantly more support than what general school settings can reasonably provide and that placement decisions should be made on an individual basis (MacMillan, Gresham & Forness, 1996). Indeed, it would seem appropriate that one consider not only the needs of the disabled student but also the needs of nondisabled peers whose learning may be adversely affected by disruptive behavior. Teachers who are not adequately prepared nor have the necessary supports available to them to help intensive needs students are also likely to be negatively affected. Quinn and Rutherford (1998) pointed out that many professional organizations involved with the education of children with disabilities (e.g., Council of Administrators of Special Education, 1994; Council for Exceptional Children, 1993; National Association of State Boards of Education, 1992) have developed position papers on the topic of full inclusion. While these organizations each promoted the notion that children with disabilities should be educated as much as possible in normal settings, they emphasized that placement decisions should also be made on an individual basis, using the full continuum of program options (Quinn & Rutherford, 1998).

What Must Be Fixed?

As discussed earlier, educators often get into arguments over whether the student needs to change or whether the system must do so. Because there are so many complicating influences in our society that impact both individuals and schools, it is unlikely that this debate will be resolved anytime soon. What we do know is that our youth with some of the most challenging behaviors often share many common characteristics. Fuller and Sabatino (1996) for example, found that students who are placed in alternative educational settings are often viewed as having antisocial attitudes and behaviors, having problematic behaviors with peers and family, and lacking academic and vocational goals. One might conclude then, that these students are "broken" because they don't fit the norm and must therefore be fixed. Clear understanding of what caused these students to be broken is not known.

However, there is also a growing understanding of what it is that makes certain alternative school models work better for disruptive youth than traditional systems. Raywid (1994) pointed out that, often, alternative educational programs rather than traditional schools, are more likely to value and promote a student's sense of belonging or connection, provide instruction that is relevant and of high interest to students and do so on a consistent basis. Fortunately, researchers who have studied school improvement processes have been able to identify key components of effective special and alternative programs for students with social, emotional and behavioral problems (Bear, Quinn & Burkholder, 2001; Osher, Dwyer & Jackson, 2004; Quinn & Rutherford, 1998).

RECENT SCHOOL INITIATIVES

As a result of the Individuals with Disabilities Education Act (IDEA, Public Law 105-17, 1997), new initiatives that focus on developing positive behavioral supports (PBS) and functional behavioral assessments (FBA) for students with emotional and behavioral disabilities have grown dramatically. While FBA's have been well known to school psychologists and others in the field of applied behavior analysis for many years, it was the mandate spelled out in IDEA that led to widespread use among other school professionals. Specifically, the amendments to the 1997 IDEA state that an FBA must be conducted for those students with disabilities whose behaviors reflect a consistent pattern of misconduct or result in a change of school placement (P.L. 105-17, (sec)615 (K)I.B.i). In its basic form, an FBA is conducted in order to determine the function of a behavior (why it occurs) and the specific circumstances under which it is most and least likely to occur (Foster-Johnson & Dunlap, 1993; O'Neil, Horner, Albin, Storey, Sprague & Newtton, 1997). The purpose of an FBA is to provide information that can lead to the development of an effective PBS plan for either an individual or on a school-wide basis.

Even for those children with the most challenging behavior, the provisions of the 1997 Amendments to the Individuals with Disabilities Act (IDEA) substantially improved the odds that they would receive an appropriate education. IDEA essentially articulated the need for schools to provide alternative means to respond to disruptive or dangerous behaviors while simultaneously addressing students' learning needs. In contrast to the basic concept of behavior management, PBS is viewed as a more proactive approach that not only responds to individual needs but also looks at altering environments that may influence challenging behaviors (Center for Mental Health in Schools, 1999; National Association of School Psychologists fact sheet, 2002; Sugai & Lewis, 1999). The fundamental purpose is to create a safe and supportive school environment while at the same time improve outcomes for all children, including those with disabilities.

The concept of PBS is more of a process than a prescribed set of practices. Ideally, it is understood as a team-based process for facilitating and maintaining student progress across settings

(Mayer, 1995; Sprague et al., 1998; Sugai & Horner, 1999). The design of systems of PBS is based on input and decision-making from every adult involved with the student, including parents. Effective interventions and supports involve four main components: 1. *Systems change* (i.e., the examination and/or improvement of organizational philosophies, policy, practices); 2. *Environmental alterations* that may occur in the classroom, school-wide or both; 3. *Skill instruction* that enhances student competencies and replaces inappropriate behaviors; and 4. *Behavioral consequences* that serve to eliminate negative behaviors (Sugai & Horner, 1999).

A key feature of all PBS plans is an understanding that outcomes are broader in scope than simply reducing behavior problems. In other words, such plans aim not only to reduce or eliminate problem behavior, but also to improve the chances that a student will succeed in various contexts (school, home, work, community). As other researchers have pointed out (Foster-Johnson & Dunlap, 1993; Horner, Dunlap, Koegel, Carr, Sailor, Anderson, Albin & O'Neill, 1990), while reducing problem behavior is certainly a primary goal, it may not be as significant without leading to real changes in the student's social, academic or vocational functioning.

Fortunately, the research on PBS programs has been encouraging in terms of its potential for improving the social-emotional, academic and vocational capabilities of students (Lewis & Sugai, 1999; Nelson, 1996; Nelson, Martella, & Garland, 1998). Numerous studies have documented the positive effects of school support and the promotion of student attachment to schools (Cox, Davidson & Bynum, 1995; Quinn & Rutherford, 1998; Wehlage, 1991). In a review of research conducted by the National Association of School Psychologists (NASP, 2002), over half of the studies that looked at the effectiveness of PBS reported a 90% reduction in disruptive behavior and almost one quarter of the studies reported complete elimination of problem behavior.

In addition to enhancing positive outcomes for individual students, PBS has also been effective when applied on a school-wide basis (Colvin & Fernandez, 2000; Scott, 2001). For example, Scott (2001) presented a case example of a school-wide PBS system that resulted in a 61% reduction in alternative room referrals for the entire school population, including minority students. In addition, the investigator reported a 65% reduction in the number of days students were suspended.

Osher, Dwyer and Jackson (2004) developed a comprehensive three-level approach to improve school discipline, safety and academic achievement. The ideas and information they provide stem from two earlier resources that were sent to every school in the United States, largely in response to the multiple shootings that occurred across the country: *Early Warning, Timely Response: A Guide to Safe Schools* (Dwyer, Osher &Warger, 1998) and *Safeguarding our Children: An Action Guide* (Dwyer & Osher, 2000). The emphasis in both of these works highlighted the need for schools to develop both strategic and comprehensive plans to combat youth violence while at the same time, address student mental health needs and school discipline. In their more recent book, entitled *Safe, Supportive and Successful Schools Step by Step* (Osher et al., 2004), the authors present a framework for school improvement efforts that considers three areas: (1) school-wide prevention programs for all students; (2) early interventions for at-risk students; and (3) more intensive interventions for students with complex emotional and behavioral disorders. A recommendation and guidelines for developing both **school-wide teams** (to address overall school performance) and **student support teams** (to address individual student behavior problems) are provided along with summaries of a number of evidence-based programs that have targeted school safety, drug and alcohol prevention, conflict resolution, child aggression, and a host of other risk and protective factors linked to mental health.

Fortunately, school improvement and safety planning efforts have been aided by many organizations at the state and federal levels. For example, Osher et al. (2004) highlighted six national resource centers that offer assistance to schools on such topics as violence prevention and school safety, barriers to learning, drug prevention, school-community partnerships and promotion of positive mental health. Those listed include: (1) the Center for Substance Abuse Prevention; (2) the Center for Mental Health; (3) the Center for Effective Collaboration and Practice; (4) the Learning First Alliance; (5) the National Coordinator Training and Technical Assistance Center for Drug Prevention and School Safety Program Coordinators; and (6) the Northwest Regional Educational Laboratory.

Programs and materials that have focused on the promotion of student's social and emotional learning competencies (SEL) have also been gaining widespread use over the past several years (Connolly, Dowd, Criste, Nelson & Tobias, 1995; Goldstein, 1988; Goldstein & Glick, 1987; Goldstein, Sprafkin & Gershaw, 1980; Mannix, 1983; McGinnis & Goldstein, 1984; Payton, Wardlaw, Graczyk, Bloodworth, Tompsett & Weissberg, 2000; Schmidt, 1997). Efforts behind many of these initiatives have been supported by various national organizations and centers. For example, the U.S. Department of Education's Safe and Drug-Free Schools Program has helped schools as they seek to learn more about what works and what programs are effective (Osher, Dwyer & Jackson, 2004). In an effort to help educators sift through the myriad of programs that are available, the Collaborative to Advance Social and Emotional Learning (CASEL) has developed a framework of key SEL skills and attitudes that students should acquire along with selection criteria for choosing quality programs. Among those competencies identified included an awareness of self and others, caring for others, responsible decision-making and effective social interaction skills (CASEL, 2000). Founded in 1994, CASEL is an international organization created to promote social and emotional learning in grades kindergarten through high school. In addition to the organization's work in identifying essential student skills and attitudes, goals also focus on curriculum design, teacher education, information dissemination and program evaluation (Payton et al., 2000).

A movement to provide more comprehensive mental health services in schools, often referred to as expanded school mental health (ESMH) programs (Weist & Christodulu, 2000), has also been gaining attention on a national level. ESMH programs are designed to augment the services provided by school psychologists and school counselors by connecting schools with community agencies including mental health, social services and other health care providers. The effort to integrate these different systems of care allows for a single point of access. Children in special and regular education may receive any number of mental health services such as prevention, assessment, case management and treatment. The model of school based mental health described by Adelman and Taylor (1993, 1999) examines key policy and programmatic issues that schools must address in their efforts to restructure systems. Adelman and Taylor serve as co-directors of the Center for Mental Health in Schools that operates under the auspices of the School Mental Health Project, Department of Psychology, UCLA. The Center is an excellent resource that offers technical assistance to schools interested in developing ESMH programs (Center for Mental Health in Schools, 2000). In principle, ESMH programs make good sense although because of numerous barriers (e.g., funding, gaps between research and practice, bureaucratic conflicts, poor communication between systems), relatively few schools have been able to implement such comprehensive programs ((Weist, 1999; Weist & Christodulu, 2000).

Related to the notion of ESMH programs has been the concept of full-service schools (Dryfoos, 1994). Full-service schools are designed as one-stop centers that address the educational, social-emotional, behavioral, health and physical needs of the child as well as the family. The intent of such schools is to reduce the barriers (e.g., transportation, insurance, flexible scheduling) to families for services they might not otherwise be able to obtain. Services are provided through collaboration among the family, school and various agencies. Often, services are also made available before and after school, on weekends and even during vacations and summers (Warger, 2001). A more complete description and guidelines for building a full-service school have been developed by Dryfoos and Maguire (2002) and Calfee, Wittwer and Meredith (1998).

Alternative programs for students with emotional, social and behavioral problems have also been in existence and for a number of years. Initially, many of these programs were designed to help students who had either dropped out or were at-risk of dropping out of school (Glass, 1994). Success in many of these programs was not simply because students were in a different location but because students were taught in a different manner. Greater flexibility is offered in terms of curriculum, scheduling and attention to individual student needs. Quinn & Rutherford (1998) described a variety of alternative programs that have been developed to serve students whose emotional and behavioral disabilities resulted in removal from the traditional school environment. Alternative programs have come under various names and models including: school-within-a-school programs, alternative schools, continuation schools, court schools, detention schools and charter schools. The literature is supportive of many of these types of alternative programs which are often better able to reach youth with severe emotional and behavioral needs (Ball, 1997; Nastasi, Varjas & Berstein, 1998).

SUMMARY

Clearly, the growing public interest in improving school safety, discipline and achievement along with a nationwide trend to reduce the barriers that thwart school improvement and access to mental health services, is encouraging. Despite continued over-use of zero tolerance policies among many schools, there is a burgeoning of resources and effective programs that are advancing our ability to improve schools and address the mental health needs of our youth. Researchers are also beginning to look at deeper contextual factors (e.g., school climate, organizational factors, financing, staff resistance to change, collaboration between mental health providers and educators) that are critical in the successful and sustainable implementation of effective programs (Atkins, Graczyk, Frazier & Abdul-Adil, 2003; Dupaul, 2003;Ringeisen, Henderson & Hoagwood, 2003). As Kazdin (2001) has pointed out, often, empirically supported treatments from controlled studies are likely to be less robust in actual clinical practice. It is not enough for a school to simply insert a program and expect it to be effective when little attention has been given to the organizational mechanisms and overall school context.

Although school-wide and early interventions for at-risk youth are providing much needed services to so many children, there is still a small percentage of children who require intensive services. It is estimated that three to five percent of students have emotional and behavioral problems that significantly interfere with their social and academic functioning (Office of the Surgeon General, 1999). Particularly for some of the most disruptive students, schools cannot just exclude those students without providing an appropriate educational program (IDEA, 1997). IDEA's guarantee of a free appropriate public education for students with disabilities, includes those students who present with some of the most challenging behaviors. Similarly, the philosophy of full inclusion of children with severe emotional and behavioral problems has been debated although many parents and professional organizations argue that traditional settings cannot sufficiently address the intensive needs of such children (MacMillan, Gresham & Forness, 1996; Quinn & Rutherford, 1998).

In response to the mandates set forth in IDEA and the struggle that school leaders often face when attempting to educate some of their most disruptive youth, there is certainly a need for practical, straightforward guidance in developing school programs. There are currently few comprehensive resources available to aid in the development and implementation of programs specific for children with intensive management needs. There is also very limited direction from federal regulations that pertains to programmatic structures and recommended interventions in nontraditional settings. A guide for the busy practitioner that focuses specifically on meeting the needs of some our most challenging students is needed. Among those questions that program developers are likely to ask might include: *What are the standards for quality programs that may not be available in a traditional setting? What might the process look like in order to effectively implement a program for disruptive youth? What resources and effective practices exist that are worth investing both time and money in?* It is the intent of this book to help answer these questions and to share pertinent information that would assist in creating systems of support for children with the most intensive needs.

CHAPTER 2

ESSENTIAL ELEMENTS OF
EFFECTIVE PROGRAMS

Effective alternative programs that serve youth with intensive emotional, learning and behavioral needs often share similar characteristics. While they may be located in area schools or in separate facilities that are more restrictive in nature (e.g., special therapeutic day schools, day treatment programs, public and private intermediary educational agencies), they provide a highly supportive community environment characterized by high performance expectations, flexibility and individual student attention (Bear et al., 2001; Cox et al., 1995; Dwyer & Osher, 2000; Quinn & Rutherford, 1998; Quinn, Osher, Hoffman & Hanley, 1998; Raywid, 1994). Programs that work and make a real difference in the lives of troubled youth are far from being the proverbial "dumping grounds" nor are they custodial in nature. Rather, they involve a highly skilled delivery of instructional and mental health services along with close collaboration with school districts. Such programs often allow students to remain in their communities and, if appropriate, transition back into their regular school districts.

For purposes of organization in this chapter, I have arranged key characteristics of effective programs into the following categories: (1) systemic features; (2) curriculum and instructional practices; (3) evidence-based interventions; and (4) comprehensive systems of support.

SYSTEMIC FEATURES

The research is very conclusive in terms identifying key features that alternative programs at a systemic level must have in order to be successful (Bear, 1999; Cox et al., 1995; Raywid, 1994; Wehlage, 1991). Listed below are those key features:

1. **Teachers who are both highly skilled and motivated to work with troubled youth.** One of the most fundamental

characteristics identified - teacher attitudes and understanding of children with serious emotional and behavioral disorders - has been a central tenet in effective programs. As mentioned earlier in Chapter One, authorities in alternative education programs have long emphasized the importance of developing a "community of support" which is vital in addressing the needs of chronic disruptive youth (Bear, 1999; Wehlage, 1991). Such "communities" generally involve a low student to teacher ratio that would allow for small group and individual instruction. Effective teachers are able to communicate a genuine degree of warmth, interest and personal respect toward students with whom they want to work. There is a sensitivity to individual and cultural differences (McIntyre, 1996). They maintain a professional attitude even during moments of behavioral disruption, student limit-testing, or more highly charged crisis situations. They are also confident and competent in their use of a variety of strategies to promote academic and social-emotional growth and value professional collaboration. Finally, they maintain their skills and often seek additional training through professional staff development opportunities.

Dr. Robert Brooks, one of the nation's leading experts on promoting self-esteem and resilience in children, has written extensively about the long-lasting impact teachers have on their students (Brooks, 1991; Brooks & Goldstein, 2001). One of the key factors that he writes about is the belief that for even some of the most troubled students, effective teachers are capable of becoming a "charismatic adult." These individuals instill a sense of self-worth in students and truly help redirect their lives. From my perspective, I would certainly agree with Dr. Brooks and others (e.g., Gottfredson, 1997; Osher et al., 2004; Quinn & Rutherford, 1998; Wehlage, 1995) who have noted that effective programs must, as a basis, have this culture of caring. A culture and a structure that helps all students succeed is a key to school success regardless of whatever technical features may exist. In my work at the Broad Street Teaching and Learning Center, our general program evaluations have always cited staff interest and commitment to students and parents as being one of the most valued features of the program.

2. **High levels of professional collaboration among faculty and staff and flexibility in programming.** Bear et al. (2001) highlighted the importance of expanded roles for teachers and other staff who are likely to serve not only as teachers, but mentors and front line counselors. Similarly, teachers and related services support staff, are highly involved with assessment, decision-making, planning and implementation of academic and mental health interventions. Collaborative problem-solving often occurs within the context of a multidisciplinary setting. School professionals are also given autonomy in reference to their ability to utilize nontraditional methods. Within the guidelines as stated in the student's individual education plan (IEP), teachers have flexibility to make adjustments in class scheduling and adaptations in curriculum, instruction and in the use of behavioral or social-emotional interventions.

3. **Funding and resources.** As most school leaders would agree, alternative programs are costly but then so are the broader human and social costs to society if we fail to intervene to address problematic student behavior. Sufficient funding not only provides an appropriate physical setting but a low student-teacher ratio, ample support staff and training, curriculum and therapy materials and technology (Bear et al., 2001). Directly related to the availability of resources is administrative support and involvement. School administrators must be actively involved in order to understand how best to allocate and utilize resources and make meaningful decisions about priorities (Sugai & Lewis, 1999). Osher et al. (2004) devote an entire chapter to the subject of funding for school improvement efforts with information and resources pertaining to federal, state, local (public) and private funding streams.

4. *On-site mental health services.* School psychologists, social workers and school counselors are a logical choice in providing a range of direct and indirect services to children, parents, teachers, other support staff and entire systems. Services often include individual and group counseling, assessment and treatment planning, advocacy and referral for community services, crisis intervention, behavioral consultation, parent education and case management, As

mentioned earlier, other staff such as teachers, teacher assistants, administrators or other related service providers may also play a direct role in supporting students whose emotional and behavioral needs demand immediate attention (Bear et al., 2001). It is important to recognize that mental health services, especially for students who are aggressive or have significant conduct disorders, must be intensive and sustained over time. Similarly, the research on effective mental health programs suggests that services need to be comprehensive (i.e., addressing multiple risk and protective factors) and broad-based (i.e., consideration of ecological or systems factors) in understanding and treating aggression (Bleckman, Prinz & Dumas, 1995; Loeber & Farrington, 1998). In addition, a key element for success is the ability of school professionals from differing perspectives to integrate mental health and educational concerns into one vision that impacts daily practice. As described by Dwyer and Osher in *Safeguarding our Children: An Action Guide,* " successful school-based mental health programs are woven into the fabric of the school including its classroom and instructional priorities" (Dwyer & Osher, 2000, p. 32).

5.   **School or program-wide behavior management systems.** Safe and effective schools have in place a clear set of expectations and rules for student conduct as well as consequences that are realistic and meaningful to all students (Bear et al., 2001; Dwyer & Osher, 2000; Sugai & Lewis, 1999). There is ongoing supervision and monitoring of behavior. Highly structured or engineered behavior management systems (e.g., token economies, level systems) are often used to reinforce positive student behaviors and help insure that staff are consistent in their disciplinary practices. As a proactive approach to discipline, such systems also serve to provide students with clear standards for appropriate behavior and frequent feedback as to their own performance. Ideally, educators, administrators, students, parents and mental health providers work collaboratively to develop these systems and other positive behavioral supports.

6.   **Continuous student and program evaluation.** Program development as well as individual student development requires ongoing feedback to refine practices and procedures.

Clearly, student progress must be regularly monitored in order to insure that the student is benefiting from instruction or therapeutic procedure and whether or not there may be a need to modify an intervention. At a systemic or program level, quantitative (i.e., data-based) and qualitative measures would be utilized to determine whether adequate progress is being made. Such data would be necessary for deciding whether to maintain, modify or discontinue any program practice. Evaluations that provide both formative and summative information are also needed to keep stakeholders (i.e., teachers, students, parents, school leaders) informed. By doing so enables these groups to make meaningful decisions, stay involved and allocate resources (Sugai & Lewis, 1999).

7.   **Transition planning.** Helping students and schools prepare for an eventual return to less restrictive settings should be the driving force of any alternative program. At the Broad Street Teaching and Learning Center, transition planning begins on day one. In this sense, we view our initial intake process as being more of an intervention than assessment component in the sense that it not only provides necessary background information but also serves to establish a beginning alliance with student, family and referring agents, a shared understanding of various member responsibilities, and development of student outcome goals. One must understand that the success of any reintegration effort into a less restrictive placement is a shared responsibility and requires close collaboration between alternative program staff, family, home district staff and agencies involved with the student.

For any successful transition to occur, there are essentially two central questions to be raised. First, how will we know when a student is ready to transition back into a less restrictive setting? What will be different? What will things look like? Secondly, what supports and services will be needed to help teach and maintain the student's new skills and generalize these to new situations? Work done at this point sets the stage for building commitment, trust and a renewed sense of hope among all members of the treatment team, including the student. To facilitate the transition planning process, and as recommended by others (Quinn & Rutherford, 1998), it would be important to ensure that transition plans and objectives are clearly stated in the student's individual education plan.

CURRICULUM / INSTRUCTIONAL FEATURES

While students referred to alternative programs require intensive mental health intervention, they typically demand intensive academic intervention as well. Many students with significant emotional and behavioral disorders are often functioning well below grade level in the areas of reading, written language and mathematics. Furthermore, they often present with significant deficits in social and daily living skills as well as in career or vocational skills (Quinn & Rutherford, 1998). Alternative programs must enable students to progress in the regular curriculum as much as possible and work toward meeting their goals as outlined in the student's IEP (IDEA, 1997).

Meaningful academic intervention can only be based on good assessment data. The use of standardized tests alone is not recommended because teachers are unlikely to use the results for instructional planning or to guide their decisions about instruction. Therefore, it is essential that educators utilize a variety of assessment measures such as reviews of the student's academic history and classroom work samples, interviews, and curriculum-based assessments.

Given the need to address a broad range of academic, social, daily living and job-related skill deficits, school officials would be wise to consider what Quinn and Rutherford have referred to as a "functional curriculum" (Quinn & Rutherford, 1998, p.22). In addition to the focus on traditional academic areas, a functional curriculum would emphasize skills necessary for daily living such as following directions, how to read a newspaper, purchase goods and services, live on a budget, use basic technology, develop basic work skills, find a job and so forth. Because the course of instruction can be disrupted by students entering and exiting programs, attendance problems or because of behavioral disruptions, more elaborate and lengthy units of study will probably be less effective. Therefore, it is recommended that programs consider using a short unit format with units that are clearly connected to each other as part of a more cohesive curriculum. Units of instruction should also be accompanied by a clear set of student outcomes or learning standards that are not only aligned with the curriculum but also agreed upon by all teachers ((Quinn & Rutherford, 1998; Waldron, 1997).

Research on effective teaching has highlighted a number of classroom characteristics and instructional practices that at-risk and other disabled students seem to benefit from (Bear et al., 2001; Brophy & Good, 1994; Ysseldyke & Christenson, 1994). Based on such findings, quality alternative programs often have the following general instructional characteristics:

- High academic expectations;
- Classroom management practices that utilize a mix of strategies such as proactive, corrective and instructive strategies;
- A highly supportive and positive classroom climate;
- A variety of instructional methods;
- Use of high interest and highly motivating materials;
- Cooperative learning opportunities;
- Active student involvement in academic and vocational planning;
- A positive and collaborative relationship with the home.

The *direct instruction* model of teaching (Engelmann, Becker & Gersten, 1988) has also been linked to improved student performance particularly for students who are not well organized, have difficulty focusing attention, are poorly motivated or are unable to monitor their own behavior effectively. Numerous studies (Adams & Engelmann, 1996; Carlson & Francis, 2002) have reported positive effects on basic academic skills, cognitive skills and affective skills. The model emphasizes teacher use of clear and detailed instructions, frequent praise and feedback, pre-teaching of vocabulary and concepts, concrete examples, high student involvement , quick pacing of oral responses, over-learning and frequent use of mastery tests to track student performance.

In addition to the direct instruction model, is other research that puts emphasis on the use of *adaptive instruction* when working with special needs children (Waldron, 1997; Waxman, Wang, Anderson & Walberg, 1985). Bear et al. (2001) provide a summary of those features involved in adaptive instruction including:

- Emphasis on teaching functional skills (i.e., daily living

and career-related skills);
- Pre-teaching of critical vocabulary and use of advanced organizers;
- Presenting clear, concrete examples of work that students will complete;
- Frequent review of material and the use of a variety of instructional formats (e.g., oral, written, audio and video, games, demonstration);
- Providing extra time to complete tasks and projects;
- Breaking learning activities into smaller units and shorter assignments;
- Using cooperative learning strategies and encouraging other student involvement through peer coaching and peer tutoring;
- Allowing flexibility for students to demonstrate mastery of learned material;
- Providing modified tests and grading.

EVIDENCE-BASED INTERVENTIONS

It should go without saying that all interventions need to be evidence-based for obvious reasons. For both ethical and outcome related reasons, schools can ill afford to waste their already limited resources on interventions that simply don't work. As such, interventions for behavioral and emotional problems must be well grounded in theory and practice. Best practice would also suggest that interventions be linked directly to assessment and that data collection should be ongoing for purposes of planning, implementing and evaluating interventions (Bear et al., 2001). In addition, practitioners must strive to ensure a goodness of fit between interventions and the unique circumstances of the school and community. Program efficacy is not necessarily a guarantee when delivered in different settings and with different populations (Weisz, Donenberg, Han & Weiss, 1995). Those who are involved with program development need to be aware of this.

Osher et al. (2004) outlined six criteria that school officials should consider when selecting interventions. These include:
- The intervention must be based on sound theory and data as to its effectiveness.

- The data must indicate a positive impact on academic achievement.
- The data must indicate effectiveness with specific student groups.
- The intervention must be capable of being incorporated within existing school structures without difficulty.
- Program developers should be able to provide necessary technical assistance.
- Program components should emphasize positive solutions to emotional and behavioral problems.

While it is beyond the scope of this book to review known effective interventions, Osher et al. (2004) provide a summary description of a number of nationally recognized interventions that have a strong research base. A variety of sources that provide information on effective practices are also listed in a separate appendix (Appendix A) at the end of this book.

COMPREHENSIVE SYSTEMS OF SUPPORT

As most mental health providers would agree, students with intensive behavioral and emotional disorders are complicated and require a system of supports and services that would be in addition to the school program. Certainly, a multitude of factors contribute to the adjustment and behavioral disorders of children including intra-individual, family, peer, and community factors (Dwyer & Gorin, 1996). In a majority of cases, it would be unreasonable to assume that the school could adequately address every need. In a recent review, for example, Bear, Webster-Stratton, Furlong, and Rhee (2000) highlighted the relationship between long-term positive outcome and parental involvement in the education and treatment of children with chronic behavior problems. Support for extended services to children and families has been advocated by mental health and other educational reform leaders for a number of years. In the *National Agenda for Achieving Better Results for Children and Youth with Emotional Disturbance* report (U.S. Department of Education, 1994), targeted objectives described the need to collaborate with families, and foster both school and community-based initiatives that would be based on the specific individual needs of at-risk and emotionally disturbed youth.

An effective approach to providing intensive expanded services has involved a "wraparound" model (Eber, 1997) that utilizes a wide spectrum of community supports and services that are tailored to the individual needs of the child and family. Supports might involve medical services, individual and family therapy, comprehensive case management, social services, respite services, crisis outreach, juvenile justice services, mentoring, and vocational training. Typically, the wraparound process involves identification and development of practical behavior plans for the student, with coordinated involvement from the student, family, school and other community professionals (e.g., mental health, social services, juvenile justice). While the development of comprehensive and coordinated systems of care is admittedly difficult to achieve, often because of competing priorities and different administrative structures between agencies, they are necessary in order to maintain the student within the community (Quinn & Rutherford, 1998). Osher et al. (2004) describe 10 essential elements of the wraparound approach that include the following:

> Individualized and strength-based assessment;
> Community-based services;
> High level of family involvement;
> Sensitivity to family and cultural contexts;
> Unconditional commitment;
> Team approach;
> Formal and informal family and community agency supports;
> Collaborative planning process involving all stakeholders;
> Flexible funding mechanisms;
> Regular monitoring of measurable outcomes.

Woodruff et al. (Woodruff, Osher, Hoffman, Gruner, King, Snow & McIntire, 1999) have identified certain key practices that enable schools to build systems of care. Among those practices include the need for having wraparound services together with school-based mental health services that provide direct support to students and families as well as teachers and administrators. School-based case management is another important component that can help in determining individual student needs, developing goals, linking children and families to community resources, monitoring the delivery of services and advocating for any necessary changes or services. Atkins et al. (2003) discussed a "new model" of school and community-based mental services in urban communities that considered accessibility, effectiveness and sustainability factors. In a series of studies that considered these factors, results clearly suggested that mental health services were significantly enhanced through reliance on indigenous community resources and that influential community members played a major role in facilitating access to mental health programs. Furthermore, families were much more likely to remain involved with school-based rather than clinic-based services alone.

Sommerville and McDonald (2002) described two models effective in developing school-community partnerships- Service Learning and Project-based Learning. Both models are designed to be "experiential, practical and connected to the real world" (Muscott, 2001). They also provide an interactive learning experience that promotes student self-esteem, a sense of caring for others, and positive interpersonal social skills. In Sommerville and McDonald's monograph (2002), we are reminded that the development of high quality school-community partnerships will take time and that what works in one school may not work in another. However, there are some general guidelines offered (cited in Liontos, 1991) that have been found helpful in working with parents and community groups to support at-risk youth. Included among the guidelines is the need to obtain strong support of the principal and staff; be flexible and creative in terms of scheduling events and problem solving; understand that home visits are necessary; be prepared to offer child care, food, and transportation; and remain committed and refuse to give up (Sommerville & McDonald, 2002).

A central theme that clearly emerges is the notion that mental health and community outreach services cannot simply be treated as an add-on, but must be an integral part of alternative school programs. This especially makes sense if our goal is to promote the necessary skills that are demanded of students so they may successfully transition into the community and world of work. Osher et al. (2004, p.118) identify a number of resources that can be used to develop intensive community-based interventions and wraparound systems of care.

SUMMARY

The challenge facing schools as they struggle to meet the intensive needs of children with emotional and behavioral disorders is not just solely that of educating these students, but, more importantly, of preparing them for successful reintegration into the workplace and community. Fortunately, the literature is replete with information helpful in the design of effective alternative school programs. Important components involving systemic factors, curriculum and instructional methods, data-based interventions and family and community supports are discussed.

Unlike their peers in traditional and less restrictive programs, students with challenging and chronic behavior problems require high quality educational instruction, mental health services and a network of community-based supports. Such programs serve as being far more than maintenance facilities or dumping grounds for undesirable students and should not be seen as an add on feature. It is understood that alternative programs are costly and require both time and sufficient resources to accomplish their goals. However, from a social, legal and ethical perspective, we also know that students who do not receive such intensive supports will likely fail to achieve any positive educational outcomes and be unsuccessful as adults.

CHAPTER 3

TEAMS AND TEAM PROCEDURES

Over the past 20 years a collaborative work environment has been consistently cited as a characteristic of effective schools, particularly as they strive to educate students with diverse needs (West, 1990; West & Idol, 1993; Will, 1986). The demand for improved student performance and accountability in the face of increasing numbers of students with disabilities has undoubtedly contributed to the push for more collaboration among professionals. This is by no means limited to schools as many corporate models stress a team approach for purposes of improving organizational effectiveness, quality of products and services and group cohesion (Nelson & Quick, 2003). Alternative school programs are no exception and demand close team collaboration among all staff in order to support student and program improvement efforts.

Collaborative partnerships that enable professionals from different fields in education, mental health and related health services to work together to improve student outcomes have proven very effective. There are a number of collaborative organizational structures within schools that fall under such names as teacher assistance teams (Chalfant, Pysh & Moultrie, 1979), intervention assistance teams (Curtis, Curtis & Graden, 1988), pre-referral teams (Graden, Casey & Christenson, 1985), child study teams and school-improvement and student support teams (Osher et al., 2004) to name only a few. Although such teams assume different titles, a common feature is that of having a school-based, problem solving unit designed to assist teachers as they struggle to develop instructional and behavioral interventions for students who are difficult to teach (Myers & Kline, 2001).

Related to the increasing trend of utilizing teams is the use of the collaborative consultation model (Idol, Paloucci-Whitcomb & Nevin, 1993). Unlike the more limited and traditional view of consultation as an expert telling others how to solve problems, a collaborative model emphasizes the interactive decision making process among professionals who share responsibility for individual student or school outcomes. Expanding on this model, West (1990) used the terms "educational collaboration" and the "collaborative school" (West & Idol, 1993) in his discussion of school-based teams. I find his description to be especially relevant to those interested in designing effective alternative school programs.

Educational collaboration is an interactive planning, decision-making, or problem-solving process involving two or more team members. The process consists of up to eight interrelated steps:

1. goal-setting
2. data collection
3. problem identification
4. alternative solutions development
5. action plan development
6. action plan implementation
7. evaluation/follow-up
8. redesign

Team interactions throughout the process are characterized by: mutual respect, trust and open communication; consideration of each issue or problem from an ecological perspective; consensual decision making; pooling of personal resources and expertise; and joint ownership of the issue or problem being addressed. The outcomes of educational collaboration may focus on changes in knowledge, skills, attitudes or behaviors at one or more of three levels: child, adult or system (West, 1990, p. 29).

Most practitioners in the field of school psychology are highly familiar with the collaborative problem-solving model (Bergan & Kratochwill, 1990) and appreciate its benefits. Certainly, the research literature supports those who would work to build a collaborative school environment that is characterized by norms of collegiality and continuous improvement (West & Idol, 1993).

Critical elements of collaborative teams have been described by Thousand and Villa (1992) who offer the following definition:

A collaborative team may be defined as a group of people who agree to:

1. coordinate their work to achieve at least one common, publicly agreed upon goal;
2. hold a belief system that all members of the team have unique and needed expertise;
3. demonstrate parity, the equal valuation of each member's input;
4. use a distributed functions theory of leadership in which the task and relationship functions of the traditional lone leader are distributed among all members of the group; and
5. employ a collaborative teaming process which involves face-to-face interaction; positive interdependence; the performance, monitoring and processing of interpersonal skills; and
6. individual accountability. (p. 76)

In their study of collaborative teams, Sharpe and Templin (1997) discuss how a team approach involves (1) shared leadership roles among teachers, administrators and other providers, (2) mutual accountability, (3) collective work products, and (4) collaborative problem-solving. Organizational team structures of this kind provide both a forum and a vehicle for educators to voice concerns, share information, gain support, and develop new strategies to improve student and/or program performance.

Investigators (Myers & Kline, 2001; Sharpe & Templin, 1997) have recognized that a team approach to student and school improvement is no easy task. No team can be effective unless it has the authority to act and the support of school leadership and the entire school community (Osher et al., 2004). It is time and effort intensive and requires a solid commitment by all members to collective performance. Lessons learned from others reveal that successful teams initially invest a large portion of their time in agreeing upon a unifying purpose. They also convert the group's purpose into clearly defined goals with specific timelines for meeting the goals and agreement with respect to the tasks expected of different members (Sharpe & Templin, 1997).

In our work at the Broad Street Teaching and Learning Center (BSTLC), we, as an entire staff, have learned that the development of a collaborative school culture is not simply a luxury, but a necessity. Nor is it something that develops over night. The benefits, however, are significant when one considers not only the development of better site programs, mental health interventions and instructional outcomes, but also improvement of teacher competencies, communication, social support for teachers and overall cost effectiveness. As has been emphasized repeatedly throughout this book, the complex needs of students who require intensive intervention demands the expertise of a diverse group of professionals who can be afforded time for collaboration. It is understood that various roles overlap and staff must therefore be flexible, open, honest and professional as they work together. Given the establishment of a collaborative school environment, the following sections highlight many of the team structures and procedures used at BSTLC that serve to address various student and system needs.

STUDENT STUDY TEAMS

Student study team meetings can be held for a variety of purposes including information sharing, problem-solving, treatment and IEP planning, progress monitoring, crisis debriefing, and family education and support. As appropriate, team members typically involve the case manager (usually the child's special education teacher), school psychologist, social worker, principal, parents, other related service providers, teacher assistants and outside agency personnel who are involved with the student.

For logistical reasons, we have found it helpful to set aside two time periods each week (following student dismissal) to be reserved for student team meetings. Any staff member can call a team meeting by scheduling it on the program's master calendar, completing a brief meeting request form and distributing it to appropriate staff. The request form includes basic information including meeting date, a brief description of the problem or concerns and goals for the meeting. Member roles and responsibilities are clearly defined. In all cases, members select a team leader who has the authority for planning and delegating responsibilities, a facilitator who has knowledge of group decision-making and observes group process, and a recorder who is responsible for taking minutes. All members are expected to actively participate in and facilitate the team process.

In addition to formal student team meetings, there is a host of other organizational structures in place -often involving mental health professionals - that occur at other scheduled times or as needed. These collaborative planning and decision-making meetings may involve the following:

- Consultation between two or more professionals (e.g., psychologist - teacher, teacher - teacher, social worker – administrator)
- Consultation between parents and school professional(s)
- Consultation with community agency professionals

STUDENT INTAKE TEAMS

Student intake teams should involve a minimum of at least three people, including a teacher, administrator and mental health professional. As in the case of student study teams, membership is determined on the basis of the individual needs of the student, including the types of services needed, community agency involvement and who the prospective teacher (i.e., the receiving teacher) will be. Each referral situation must be reviewed on a case-by-case basis to ensure that the program can provide sufficient help, quality services and instruction to meet the needs of the child and his or her family. From an ethical standpoint, every effort must be made to insure objectivity in decision making in order to advocate for the best interests of children and their families. In this regard, it is important for any program to identify criteria or factors that should be taken into consideration prior to acceptance into the program.

At BSTLC, we have found it helpful to carefully examine the following six factors as part of our decision-making process at intake:

- Least restrictive placement – What other treatment options or interventions have been attempted to this point? Have all other less restrictive options been exhausted?
- Safety concerns – Does the child present as a significant danger to himself or others? Is the student actively suicidal or homicidal?

- Student characteristics – This would include a clear statement indicating reason for referral and review of current educational, psychological, medical and social history records.
- District and family commitment to program – What level of cooperation can we expect and how invested are the family and/or referring school district in engaging in the treatment process? Is there congruence of goals involving all parties?
- Goodness of fit – Is there space available in the program? How will the student respond to the current classroom dynamics and milieu?
- Staffing – Is there appropriate staffing to meet the child's needs and provide the recommended educational service levels?

A critical feature of the BSTLC intake process is the emphasis on family and referring agency involvement. At the onset, this process lays the foundation for future collaborative interaction between the student's family, the home school (referring agency), and the program. The intake procedure follows a five-step process that involves the following:

1) Informal inquiry (e.g., telephone) from a referral agency as to the appropriateness of program placement and whether any openings are available;
2) Review of written student records by each member of the intake team;
3) Separate interviews involving the student, family and referring agency personnel followed by a tour of the program;
4) A follow-up team meeting of BSTLC staff that serves to summarize the student's situation with a final decision regarding admission;
5) The program administrator discusses the team's decision with the referring agency along with any other recommendations. Start dates are determined and additional communication occurs with the family who receives an admission packet to review.

In an effort to maximize efficiency in our data collection and decision-making process, we have found it helpful to conduct student, family and referring agency interviews separately and concurrently. As a general rule, the program administrator and teacher(s) meet with referring agency staff while the psychiatrist meets with the student and school psychologist or social worker interview the parents. As part of that interview, the parents are provided with a more detailed description of the program including the program philosophy, student and family expectations and range of services offered. Information obtained from all three interviews and other supporting data are discussed (usually later that same day) in a follow-up meeting with all team members. Initial short-term treatment goals, interventions and other service recommendations are then established.

SPECIAL PURPOSE TEAMS

Special purpose teams, by their very nature, are often formed to address specific issues such as academic performance, school safety, student support or school management. Teams should not have overlapping functions nor should they focus on multiple symptoms. In both situations, such teams would be likely to consume valuable leadership resources, time and money.

Attention should also be given to the process of member selection and individual member characteristics. For example, how will you recruit and maintain members? Will your team include community members and, if so, how will they be found? How will the team leadership be selected? Osher et al. (2004) suggest that teams should "have five assets – knowledge, perspective, technical skills, personal skills and legitimacy" (p.15). Team members should be knowledgeable about the program and, ideally, at least some should be knowledgeable about mental health, school safety, curriculum, instruction and student support. Members should be representative of different stakeholder perspectives that make up the entire school program. Some members should have the technical skills that would be necessary to complete certain team objectives (e.g., data analysis, grant writing). All members should possess the ability to relate in a positive fashion with each other and should be respected by other members of the school (program) community.

At BSTLC, some of our special purpose teams have

included an advisory team, safety committee team and quality assurance team, to name only a few. The advisory team functions in many respects as a central governing body for the program. Other individuals or groups are invited to share their ideas, concerns and recommendations to the advisory team. In turn, the team serves to "advise" the principal on matters of program management and program improvement. For example, topics of discussion might include school climate, improving organizational efficiency, implementation of new programs, curriculum and staffing, or other resource needs. As it's name implies, the safety team addresses those matters involving safety and emergency procedures, building security, student safety drills (fire, lockdown) and building inspections. Both teams meet regularly and on a monthly basis. The quality assurance team meets quarterly to review behavioral records, student and staff incidence reports, and other data that would be pertinent to quality of care and behavior management issues.

CRISIS INTERVENTION TEAMS

Whether one wishes to acknowledge it or not, crisis situations will develop in alternative programs and it is essential that staff are prepared to address these situations. Any response to crisis intervention should be based on a team approach for important reasons. From a logistical perspective, often there are multiple tasks that must be attended to (e.g., leading the intervention, removing bystanders, rearranging the environment, seeking additional assistance) that would require a minimum of two or more people. Caraulia and Steiger (1997) highlight three benefits of team intervention including: safety, professionalism, and support in cases that may go to litigation. The safety of everyone involved in a crisis situation is paramount and a team of professionals is likely to handle a physically acting out individual more safely than a single person would be able to do. Team members are also more likely to lend support to one another. This, in turn, can reduce the chances of any personal power struggle from occurring and, subsequently, reduce the likelihood that a staff member will overreact to the situation. Because the potential for litigation is always possible, a team approach provides an important advantage because another person is on the scene – a witness. When compared with a solo intervention, a team intervention is also more likely to have used a less restrictive method – using the least amount of force necessary.

The BSTLC program utilizes the Crisis Prevention Institute Model (CPI) that emphasizes use of a nonviolent team approach in crisis situations (Crisis Prevention Institute, 1988). While there are a number of other approaches designed to address seriously disruptive and dangerous behavior (e.g., CALM Training, 1997; Professional Assault Response Training, 2002; Satori Alternatives to Managing Aggression, 1999; SCIP-R Training: NYS Office of Mental Retardation & Developmental Disabilities, undated; Therapeutic Crisis Intervention: Residential Child Care Project, Family Life Development Center, 2002), my experience and ideas are based largely on the CPI model. As a site trainer and instructor with the Crisis Prevention Institute for over 15 years, I have had firsthand experience instituting this approach at BSTLC and in numerous other educational settings. Chapter Seven will provide a more in depth look at crisis management guidelines and procedures.

TRANSITION PLANNING TEAMS

As mentioned earlier in this chapter, planning for discharge should begin at the time of initial intake. In other words, staff should begin with the end in sight. This is a point in time during which long-term goals can be established, interventions agreed upon and other community services for both the child and family (e.g., family therapy, respite care, crisis support) can be put into place.

Discharge planning teams operate in a similar fashion to the student study teams. Typically, members include the case manager (generally, the child's special education teacher), a school psychologist or social worker, administrator, parents, the student and representatives from the student's home school district or other placement facility that will be receiving the student. Based on the student's performance and overall level of readiness, the child's teacher and counselor initially make a recommendation for discharge and reintegration into a less restrictive setting. This sets the stage for future classroom observations and meetings with home district staff that provide the case manager with critical information about features of the new setting. Such information is likely to include details about the following: (1) curriculum materials and instructional methods; (2) teacher expectations and classroom rules; (3) behavioral intervention strategies and available supports. Together, this information is then shared with the discharge team (i.e., student, parents and program staff) who integrate this into the student's school routine. On occasion, the prospective teacher from the home school may also visit the alternative program site in order to meet the student and learn more about instructional and behavioral strategies that have been effective with the student.

Following initial contacts between the case manager and home school, an arrangement is made for the student to visit the new setting for either a partial or full day. This enables the student to become familiar with the school environment and have an opportunity to meet teachers, the principal, counseling staff and peers. Once visitation(s) has been completed, the discharge team meets to insure that the necessary supports are in place for successful reintegration. A formal discharge date is determined and a celebration is planned in recognition of the student's success in the program.

BSTLC program data regarding student success following discharge have been encouraging. On an annual basis over the past ten years, approximately one-third of the student population transitions into a less restrictive setting. Recent informal follow-up inquiries at one-year post discharge indicate that approximately 90% of the students have been successful as defined by their academic and behavioral performance, attendance, and school participation. In many instances, students were unsuccessful because they failed to receive the recommended supports and services in their home school. This points to the necessity to attend closely to detail and strengthen commitments when working collaboratively with team members.

Our process at BSTLC is similar to another excellent model, entitled *The Positive Education Program: Reintegration Model* that has been used at the West Shore Day Treatment Center in Cleveland, Ohio (Quinn & Rutherford, 1998, p.39). A unique feature of the West Shore model is the responsibility that is placed on the student who declares a readiness to exit the program with a "petition for graduation." The student must be able to acknowledge past behaviors that led to initial placement, describe areas of improvement and discuss how he or she will cope with problematic situations in the future. Another positive feature is the attention placed on building a support system in the new setting that involves the identification of a building advocate. The advocate helps monitor the student's adjustment, ensures that intervention plans are followed, assists in crisis situations and serves as a main contact between the home setting and alternative program. Program data regarding successful reintegration status at one-year follow-up was highly positive. When compared with a national average of only 20% success (Groesnick, George, George & Lewis, 1991), 85% of the students from the West Shore program maintained their success during the first year in their home school (Quinn & Rutherford, 1998).

SUMMARY
        Programs designed to educate students with intense emotional and behavioral needs require the expertise of all members of the school community who can work together supported by a culture of mutual respect. Without strong partnerships within the school and community, it would be impossible to adequately address the complexity of student and family needs. As described in this chapter, specific tasks involving intake procedures, behavior assessment and management, crisis intervention, transition planning and program operations are well suited for a collaborative team approach. Simply stated, we can accomplish much more together than we can alone.
        In addition to improved outcomes for students, teams and teamwork also provide important benefits to staff – psychologically and technically. A collaborative school environment is more likely to enhance staff morale, commitment to change efforts and create a greater sense of pride and accomplishment. It is also more likely to create a safer environment and promote improvement with respect to instructional and behavior management skills.

CHAPTER 4

UNDERSTANDING AND ASSESSING STUDENT BEHAVIOR

A general characteristic of many students who exhibit serious mental health problems and antisocial behavior is that they have not developed self-awareness and management skills to an age appropriate level. There are many reasons why these students engage in behavior that is dangerous, ineffective and destructive. Because of early life experience, many have developed patterns of behavior that have become highly effective as a method of gaining negative attention. For some, violent, explosive behavior is the result of experiences of maltreatment and abuse or distorted perceptions of surroundings. For still others, it may relate to neurological dysfunction, and for others, from an attempt to hide their feelings of vulnerability and helplessness (Bridge, Gallagher, Livermon, Nusbaum & Bierman, 1986). To assist students in the process of developing self-management and effective coping skills, interventionists must not only seek to eliminate problem behaviors but also arm students with new skills that foster academic, behavioral and social competence.

Consultants who are called upon to help design behavioral interventions must have a number of skills that are in addition to their content knowledge of effective, research-based strategies. As Curtis, Zins & Graden (1987) have identified, effective behavioral consultants must also be keen observers, skilled problem-solvers, and good negotiators who can match interventions that address both the student's needs as well as the teacher's needs with consideration to the entire classroom ecology in which the teacher functions. As noted by Cohen and Fish (1993), if school practitioners are to design effective interventions that benefit troubled students, they will need to look beyond a traditional person-centered model of maladjustment and consider "organizational and systems (environmental) variables" that contribute to the psychological distress experienced by students

53

(see Elias and Branden, 1988, for their review of person-centered and environment-centered approaches). An ecological or systems perspective is particularly well matched to school practice for several reasons. First, it enables the practitioner to move away from a focus on individual psychopathology and, instead, consider the needs of the child and the resources available in the school. Second, consultation is more likely to become a shared, collaborative process because the practitioner is not attempting to help the teacher "cure" the sick child but to improve his or her effectiveness in working with the child. Finally, the focus of the intervention relates directly to the setting where the behavior must ultimately occur (Cohen & Fish, 1993).

In this context, the following sections describe various strategies with demonstrated value for working with troubled children in school settings. It is must be understood that the use and design of any management procedure respects the individual needs and dignity of all students. Judicious use of any strategy must also take into account multiple factors that would include the student's age, degree of parental involvement, teacher skill, ethical/moral considerations, and the extent of administrative support. Ultimately, there must be assurance that the treatment is in the child's best interest and that any intervention be competently conducted and effective. In addition to parents and teachers, children also have a right to participate in decisions about their treatment as much as possible.

Students who present with severe and/or chronic patterns of problem behavior are more likely to improve when there are positive school-wide and classroom systems of behavior management in place. Also, the development and implementation of individual supports should occur in a comprehensive and collaborative manner involving the student (if possible) and people who know him/her best. Clearly, the goal is to reduce problem behavior while increasing a student's adaptive skills and chances for a better quality of life. Any intervention should involve a process of functional behavioral assessment (FBA) and a behavioral intervention support plan. The individualized support plan should include a number of options such as: (1) instruction for the student in how to use new skills to replace problem behaviors, (2) modifying antecedent and consequent events to prevent problems and reinforce more positive behaviors, (3) a safety or crisis plan for severe behavioral episodes, and (4) procedures for evaluating the plan's effectiveness (www.pbis.org/tertiaryPrevention.htm).

FUNCTIONAL ASSESSMENT AS AN INTEGRAL COMPONENT TO TREATMENT PLANNING

The link between assessment and intervention for problem behavior is obvious and an understanding of student needs should be an essential function of most alternative programs. Best practice clearly indicates that the design of any worthwhile intervention must be based on useful data collected from the natural environment. The goal of functional assessment is basically twofold: First, to clarify understanding of a student's behavior using descriptive, observable terminology that identifies a behaviors' purpose in the context of the environment; and secondly, to increase the likelihood of developing a practical and effective intervention. A functional behavioral assessment (FBA) that attempts to identify factors that explain *why* a student's behavior occurs can provide such data and should be a first step in treatment planning. In general terms, an FBA includes the following features: (1) it involves direct and indirect assessment methods; (2) it addresses the student's problem within the setting in which it occurs; (3) it provides information necessary to develop interventions; and (4) it allows for ongoing monitoring of a student's behavior (Halpren & Fuhrer, 1984).

Given these features, it is understandable why FBA procedures were included within the 1997 amendments to the Individuals with Disabilities Act (IDEA). As mentioned earlier in this text, the discipline provisions of IDEA specify that a student's individual education plan must consider the use of positive behavioral interventions and supports. These, in turn, must be based on results from an FBA.

It has been recognized that IDEA '97 does not specify the theoretical foundation nor does it list the components of an FBA (Gresham, Watson & Skinner, 2001; Nelson, Roberts, Bullis, Albers & Ohland, 2000). Consequently, practitioners have developed very different perspectives on this subject with some focusing strictly on environmental causes of behavior (e.g., the applied behavior analysis model) and others looking at multiple influences (Bear et al., 2001; Nelson et al., 2000). In order to increase the power of any treatment plan, I rely more heavily on this broader problem-solving perspective that goes beyond the search for causal environmental events that are functionally related to the target behaviors. While it would be important to understand this functional relationship, it would also be important to identify the individual's strengths, limitations, interests, social skills and motivation in relation to the environmental demands and supports available to him or her.

FBA's are probably more effective when approached as a collaborative rather than expert-driven process. As mentioned earlier, a support team that is responsible for assessment and intervention should ideally include the student, the student's family, teachers and other direct support personnel who know the student best and have expertise in applied behavior analysis. They should also include people who not only have a vested interest in helping the student but are also present in those environments in which the student participates.

Successful behavioral interventions are generally a result of well-conducted FBA's. To conduct a thorough FBA most practitioners engage in the following activities:

1. *Identification / definition of target and replacement behaviors.* This should be stated in observable and measurable terms and yield a reliable measure of student performance.

2. *Review pertinent information from records reviews and previous interventions.*

3. *Interview all significant persons including teachers, assistants, administrators, related service providers, parents and student (if appropriate) who are directly involved with the student.*

4. *Observe and identify factors within the physical setting that may influence student behavior (i.e., reinforce problem behavior or block the replacement behavior).* Such factors could include curriculum or task demands, social interactions, teacher characteristics, noise, etc.

5. *Collect baseline data for the occurrence of the target behavior.* This may involve measures of frequency, intensity or duration.

6. *Identify specific antecedent events and the consequences that follow.* When, where, and with whom does the target behavior occur most often? Least often?

7. *Identify the purpose or function of the behavior.* Is the behavior indicative of a skill deficit? Does the behavior occur in an effort to gain attention or a desired item or activity, avoid a task, escape from demands, control a situation, communicate a need or desire, or receive self-stimulatory sensations?

8. *Hypothesize ways to manipulate the antecedents in order to reduce or eliminate the targeted behavior.* Identify reinforcers to increase positive replacement behaviors.

While it is well beyond the scope of this book to describe the various approaches to conducting FBAs, there are many excellent resources on this topic that provide in-depth information (see Center for Effective Collaboration and Practice, 1998; Crone & Horner, 2003; Gresham & Lambros, 1998; Kaplan, 2000; O'Neill, Horner, Albin, Storey & Sprague, 1997; Sattler, 2001; Shapiro& Kratochwill, 2000). There is also an extensive list of websites offering information on functional assessment that can be located through any search engine by entering the key words – functional behavioral assessment and behavior intervention plans. Recommended sites include the following: NASP (www.naspweb.org), the Center for Effective Collaboration and Practice (http://cecp.air.org/), and the Parent Advocacy Coalition Educational Rights (www.pacer.org/parent/function.htm).

SUMMARY

Prior to the design and implementation of any behavioral management plan there must be a clear understanding of specific factors that may be contributing to the problem as well as an understanding of student needs. Functional behavioral assessment is described as being a key link in this process because it helps to explain problem behavior and provides information necessary to develop interventions.

An ecological versus person-centered perspective to problem understanding is described and seen as being particularly well suited for school applications because it relates directly to the resources and setting where the behavior occurs. In addition, an ecological perspective is more likely to involve a collaborative effort between the practitioner and other key staff to identify the most effective methods for working with the student rather than seeking a "cure." The design of any effective intervention will most likely be based on the ideas of various individuals who know the student best, have a vested interest in helping the student and are also present in the student's environment.

CHAPTER 5

INDIVIDUAL STUDENT
BEHAVIOR MANAGEMENT

Very often, individual behavior improvement plans are necessary in order to address specific requests for help from teachers and/or parents. They often complement other group management systems (e.g., classroom management plans) that provide a foundation for individual support. For students who need a greater degree of individualization, it may be necessary to develop new strategies or adapt portions of an existing group management system (e.g., behavioral expectations, reward schedules, physical arrangement, type and amount of reward) in order to meet their unique needs.

Any individualized behavioral plan should not only focus on decreasing behaviors of concern, but also promoting adaptive or replacement skills that can lead to a better quality of life. Behavioral goals can relate to any number of areas for intervention including:

- increasing school participation and attendance
- developing and maintaining significant relationships
- increasing personal skills and expertise
- fostering independence and self-sufficiency

GUIDELINES FOR DEVELOPING SUCCESSFUL MANAGEMENT PLANS

In order to maximize the success of any management plan, there are a few guiding principles that should be considered. For example, whenever possible, the design and selection of any intervention should be a collaborative process involving the referring staff member (i.e., teacher) and student, if appropriate. As Rathvon (1999) pointed out in her comprehensive text on school interventions, "teachers need to feel that they have ownership of the solution to the problem, not just ownership of the problem" (p. 28). In and of itself, no intervention will be effective. All parties must have a shared investment in the intervention. Another principle relates to the concept of treatment acceptability and how easily it can be implemented given the time and resources needed. Particularly for teachers who feel overwhelmed, it is often best to design simple interventions that require minimal modifications in current instructional or behavioral management routines. Finally, treatment integrity – the degree to which a planned intervention is implemented as it was intended – is often assumed rather than assessed (Gresham, 1989). All too often, school practitioners rely on a "consult and hope" approach where they consult with teachers and then hope that teachers will implement the procedures with integrity. To address this issue, Gresham (1989) makes the following suggestions:

- Put the plan in writing. Plans should spell out the specific responsibilities of all participants with detailed descriptions of the intervention.
- Provide training for teachers and students in the intervention methods. This should include an explanation as to the purpose of the intervention, review and practice of the intervention techniques, and feedback to teachers and students on how well they followed the procedures.
- Periodically, observe the teacher (consultee) during early implementation stages and provide corrective feedback to ensure treatment integrity.
- Keep the intervention simple. Overly complex and ecologically intrusive interventions are difficult to implement and will only serve to create an additional burden for the teacher.

STAGES IN PLAN DEVELOPMENT
        The following steps that are outlined below are adapted from a number of resources (National Association of School Psychologists [NASP], 1986; Rathvon, 1999; Wielkiewicz, 1986; Zins, Curtis, Graden & Ponti, 1988) and they have relevance for individual consultants as well as for student study teams.
Stage 1: Problem Definition
    a) *Initial referral.* The process begins with a request for assistance that should be completed in written format to insure that all necessary information is included.

b) *Parent and student conference.* Staff should arrange to meet with the parents (and student, if appropriate), to inform them of the referral and seek their assistance in terms of understanding the problem and identifying any possible solutions.

c) *Clarify problem definition.* Problem behavior needs to be specified in very concrete, measurable terms in order to obtain adequate measurement data and determine fairly easily whether the target behavior has or has not occurred. Vague or global behavioral labels (e.g., aggressive, hyper, depressed, etc.) are not helpful because they do not specify what behavior occurring under what circumstances will receive consequences (Wielkiewicz, 1986). In addition to the establishment of a clear definition of the target behavior, consensus should also be reached on the desired outcomes. Ideally, selection of any behavior change goals should be done carefully, and if possible, in collaboration with the student. Inappropriate behaviors to be reduced as well as replacement behaviors need to be specified.

d) *Collection of baseline data.* One or more measures of the target behavior (e.g., frequency or rate of occurrence) are obtained prior to the beginning of the program. This helps define the discrepancy between the student's current level of performance and the desired level of performance. Baseline data provides the standard against which the success of the management plan can be judged. Once the program begins, data would continue to be collected using the same observational methods.

Stage 2: Problem Analysis

e) *Examining ecological factors.* As in an FBA process, multiple influences including home, classroom, curriculum, peer and community factors may be contributing to the problem.

f) *Generating possible intervention strategies.* Alternative intervention strategies can be explored at this point with input from as many sources as possible. Any strategy, however, should be evaluated for acceptability, efficacy, cost, practicality and how well it matches teacher, student or parent needs.

g) *Intervention selection.* After consideration of important treatment factors mentioned above, one or more strategies can be selected with the final decision resting with the person who will be responsible for implementing the intervention.

h) *Developing the written plan.* A detailed written plan would be developed that would include a description of the strategy or strategies to be used along with the necessary human and material resources and timelines for implementation. The behavior plan would also include a description of the roles and responsibilities of all parties involved, duration of the plan and evaluation methods for determining the overall effectiveness of the plan. Figure 1 provides an example of what the plan may look like.

Stage 3: Implementation

i) *Beginning the intervention.* The teacher and/or parent begin implementing the plan. The consultant would be available to observe in an effort to assess treatment integrity and provide helpful feedback.

Stage 4: Evaluation

j) *Determining intervention effectiveness.* Following the implementation of the behavioral plan, data would be collected again and compared with that obtained during baseline. Records would be kept to document progress and make any revisions if necessary. Effective treatments produce measurable changes in behavior. All interventions should include objective methods for evaluating outcomes and determining whether any adjustments are necessary if progress is not evident over a certain period of time.

k) *Follow up monitoring and referral.* If the plan is not succeeding, further problem solving would occur with a review of the original plan and another cycle through the steps in plan development. Additional information used in problem solving may be necessary and, if further attempts to resolve the problem fail, a referral for some other form of assistance may be appropriate (Rathvon, 1999).

Figure 1 - Behavior Plan Summary Sheet

BEHAVIOR PLAN SUMMARY SHEET		
Date		
Student(s)	Age:	Grade:
Teacher(s)		
Other Participants		
Goal(s):		
Date	Action(s)	Responsibility
Evaluation		

It is not the intent of this book to offer an exhaustive list of specific interventions for every problem behavior, although a few common strategies will be described. As one would expect, there are numerous other resources available that provide excellent and detailed descriptions of interventions to help children with learning, emotional and behavioral problems.   Some of my favorite references include the following: (1) *Handbook of school-based interventions: Resolving student problems and promoting healthy educational environments,* by J. Cohen and M. Fish (1993); (2) *The well-managed classroom,* by T. Connolly, T. Dowd, A. Criste, C. Nelson and L. Tobias (1995); (3*) Children's solution work,* by I. K. Berg and T. Steiner (2003); (4) *Effective school interventions: Strategies for enhancing academic achievement and social competence,* by N. Rathvon (1999); (5) *Interventions: Collaborative planning for students at-risk,* by R. Sprick, M. Sprick and M. Garrison (1993).   Each of these are listed in the reference section to this book.   In addition, there is an extensive list of periodicals and professional journals that provide the reader with current, research-based descriptions of both individual and group-based interventions (e.g., *Behavioral Interventions, Behavioral Disorders, Behavior Modification, Journal of Emotional and Behavioral Disorders, Preventing School Failure, School Psychology Review)* and web sites of many helpful national resources are listed in Appendix A at the back of this book.   Regardless of the specific intervention to be used, each one should be designed and implemented with full recognition of the following features as highlighted by Sprick et. al (1993):

- Students must be treated with dignity and respect for their differences.
- A focus should be on teaching skills for success.
- Positive interventions should be used to encourage responsibility and motivation.
- Behavior to be corrected provides a teaching opportunity.
- Staff collaboration is critical in responding to student needs.

Contingency Management

Contingency management represents a broad range of behavioral intervention procedures that involve either the awarding or withdrawing of rewards or punishments in order to alter the behavior that precedes these consequences (Goldstein & Keller, 1987).   Basically, it consists of two core strategies.   The first is designed to increase the frequency of desired behaviors by delivering a reinforcing agent (e.g., social, activity, material, token) contingent upon the display of such behavior.   The second, designed to decrease the frequency of inappropriate behaviors, involves punishment that is most often in the form of removal of positive reinforcers (e.g., extinction, time out, response cost) or the introduction of aversive stimuli (reprimands, overcorrection, restitution). Whether you are attempting to increase or decrease a specific behavior, the consequences must be important and mean something to the individual. Taking or giving something that isn't of any interest to the student will not help change the behavior you want to change.

There is an exhaustive research base that has successfully demonstrated the effectiveness of contingency management strategies used in modifying aggressive or severely deviant behavior across various populations (Ayllon & Azrin, 1968; Ayllon & Michael, 1959; Lovaas, Koegel, Simmons & Long, 1973; Schwitzgebel, 1964). Briefly, I will review some of the primary contingency management methods that became more widely used in the 1960's and 1970's with children and adults in hospitals, clinics and school settings. As previously discussed, the use of any contingency management procedure would first require a clear understanding of the goal(s) to be accomplished. Additional preparation would involve identification of potential reinforcers and the optimal contingency management procedure to be used.

Positive Reinforcement. A basic principle of contingency management is the belief that the introduction of any reinforcing event contingent upon the occurrence of a given behavior will increase the likelihood of that same behavior occurring again. The research is very clear on those factors that influence the success or power of reinforcement when used to increase a behavior. Major factors include the following:

- *Be Contingent.* Although this may seem largely obvious, it is critical to ensure that the connection between the target behavior and subsequent reward is made clear and explicit.
- *Reinforce Immediately.* Reinforcement that is presented immediately or as soon as possible following the desired behavior is likely to have a more powerful effect. An immediate versus delayed reinforcement presentation also reduces the risk that another behavior (i.e., an undesirable behavior) will inadvertently be reinforced.

- *Reinforce Consistently.* Because the effects of positive reinforcement tend to result in gradual rather than dramatic behavior change, it is important to maintain a consistent effort over time. Ideally, this same reinforcement effort should be similar across different settings.
- *Rate or Frequency of Reinforcement.* A very high or continuous rate of reinforcement is generally needed to establish new behaviors. Once a target behavior has been acquired, the reinforcement schedule can then be "thinned" using a partial or variable delivery strategy that can help strengthen and sustain performance.
- *Amount of Reinforcement.* The amount of reinforcement available tends to have a greater impact on performance than on learning. That is, regardless of the size of reward, individuals are likely to learn new skills and behaviors at about the same rate. In contrast, an individual's performance is more likely to be strengthened with larger rewards. If the reward becomes too large, however, a satiation effect can occur in which the individual loses interest in what was once a reinforcing event. Nevertheless, I often encourage contingency managers not to be stingy with the amount of the reward they deliver. When the amount of reward is too small, the person will soon lose interest in working to obtain it. The most appropriate method of determining the optimal amount of any reward would be through empirical means that involves observation to see whether the reinforcement is yielding the desired effect. If an individual has worked in the past to obtain a reward but no longer seems interested, you may be seeing a satiation effect. In such instances, the amount of reward should be reduced. Conversely, if you suspect that the individual may desire a particular reinforcer but is unwilling to work for such a reward, you might test this out be delivering the reward non-contingently once or twice. If the individual seems to enjoy the reward, you might then want to increase the amount in order to effect behavioral change.
- *Variety of Reinforcement.* Just as too much of a good thing can lead to a satiation effect, similar problems can arise when the same reinforcer is used repeatedly. In many instances, it can be helpful to provide a menu of reinforcers or use a random delivery schedule.

- *Rewarding Approximations.* In many cases, it would be unrealistic to expect an individual to display a new target behavior if that behavior is not already in the person's behavioral repertoire. For example, if a student interrupts others inappropriately and at a high frequency rate, it is unlikely that you will see the desired behavior emerge simply because you identified it as a target goal. What would be more reasonable might be to teach the specific steps used in the skill of interrupting appropriately and then reinforce those behaviors that gradually approximate the desired skill (e.g., standing near the person, waiting to be acknowledged, saying "Excuse me for interrupting," etc.). The process of reinforcing closer approximations or "behavioral shaping" is especially needed when the individual is learning to acquire new behaviors that would not otherwise emerge.

Withdrawing Positive Reinforcement. Effective behavior change efforts often require the presentation of reinforcement for appropriate behavior as well as the removal of reinforcement in response to undesirable behavior. In many instances, both processes occur simultaneously to increase the power of the intervention. Some of the more common strategies that are specifically designed to remove positive reinforcement include:

- *Extinction.* Extinction is a process involving the removal of positive reinforcement for undesirable behavior that has been either deliberately or inadvertently reinforced in the past (Goldstein & Keller, 1987). There have been a number of investigators who have demonstrated the effectiveness of extinction as a method used to reduce inappropriate behaviors (Jones & Miller, 1974; Madsen, Becker & Thomas, 1968; Ward & Baker, 1968). Particularly in response to milder forms of aggressive or disruptive behavior and when others are not in jeopardy of any danger, extinction may be a good choice for a strategy. Efforts to reduce inappropriate behavior by extinction should always be countered through tandem efforts by reinforcing other appropriate behavior. Ideally, the inappropriate and appropriate behaviors would be opposites or at least incompatible with one another. For example, if you wanted to decrease the frequency of talking out without permission, you could reinforce appropriate hand-raising while ignoring the student's blurting out behavior.

An initial step is to identify the reinforcers that are maintaining inappropriate behaviors.   By conducting a functional behavioral assessment, it would be essential to determine what the individual is working for, hoping to gain or otherwise receiving (i.e., the reinforcement) via his/her disruptive behavior.   Very often, as in the case of verbal aggression and mild forms of disruption, the student is gaining attention from both peers and adults either by being looked at, spoken to, or laughed at.   In addition to identifying the reinforcing agent that is maintaining the disruptive behavior, behavior managers must ensure that they are consistent over time in their application of this strategy.   This also requires that anyone within the target person's environment work together in concert to withdraw reinforcement or attention in response to inappropriate behavior.

As a final note, one must be prepared to use extinction for a sufficient length of time. Certainly, aggressive and disruptive behaviors often have a long history of being reinforced – usually on an intermittent schedule – and it will take time to create noticeable change. I often urge behavior managers to maintain their extinction efforts for a period of at least one to two weeks.   In addition, a behavior manager should be prepared early on for the possibility of an "extinction burst" (Goldstein & Keller, 1987) when extinction is first introduced. It is often common to see an increase in the rate or intensity of inappropriate behavior before it gradually declines. Although this can be seen as discouraging, it is often a good sign that your extinction efforts are having a positive effect.

- *Time Out.* Time out is a procedure involving the removal of all reinforcers for a specific period of time in response to aggressive or other disruptive behavior.   Its purpose is to reduce or eliminate inappropriate behavior by removing the individual from the reinforcing situation or by removing the individual's access to reinforcement. Successful time outs are often a result of two important factors: (1) a rich or highly positive time in environment and (2) consistent use of the time out procedure (Ewing, 2000).   Time out will only be effective if the environment from which the student is removed consists of desirable tasks and social interactions and when used in conjunction with a behavior management program that teaches and reinforces acceptable behaviors. As a behavior reduction strategy, it is probably best used with children ages 2 to 12 who are engaging in high rates of aggressive behavior that is potentially dangerous to themselves and others. For many students at the upper middle school and high school levels, time out and physical removal by an adult is neither appropriate, wise or even possible (Goldstein & Keller, 1987). Other procedures to be discussed later would be more appropriate for this age group.

Despite what many people may believe, time out is not simply the act of moving an individual to a secluded setting. This may be an accurate description of isolation, but it is by no means the only way in which time out can be applied. Gast and Nelson (1977) describe three classical variations of time out including:

1) Sit and Watch – The adult places the student in a position of contingent observer. The student sits where others can be observed engaging in an instructional activity. The student, however, may not participate in the activity. Time limits are generally brief (e.g., 30 to 60 seconds).

2) Exclusionary Time Out – The student is directed to sit in an area in the classroom from which he/she cannot observe others (e.g., behind a partition). The student is denied access to reinforcement by being removed from an ongoing activity. Maximum effective time is up to two minutes.

3) Isolation or Seclusionary Time Out – The student is removed from the instructional setting or placed in an isolation room (e.g., seclusion or safe room) that is completely separate from the main classroom or activity setting. Time periods may go up to five minutes with 20 to 30 minutes as a maximum. The student's exit from time out should be contingent upon the child being settled or compliant.

First and foremost, the use of isolation time out should only be considered as part of a continuum of behavioral interventions and never be used in isolation. Parent/guardian consent should be obtained before using seclusionary time out as an intervention. The potential use of a time out room should be addressed in the student's individual education or 504 plan and data kept routinely in an effort to monitor the effectiveness of the procedure in decreasing specified behaviors. As a minimum, the behavior record or time out log would include the child's name, factors precipitating the time out intervention, the time the student entered and exited time out, the student's behavior at time of exit and the name or initials of staff involved in the intervention. What is important to recognize is that time out is *not* an educational program. If a student is spending excessive amounts of time in isolation to the detriment of his/her educational program, it may be an indication that the current educational program be reviewed.

Time out in the classroom would be appropriate when a student's behavior begins to interfere with classroom functioning and cannot be diffused by means of redirection, physical proximity control, humor, positive reinforcement, natural consequences, etc. Time out would not be appropriate if the child sees it as an escape (e.g., the child acts out physically during reading in order to be placed in time out which then becomes rewarding to the child).

During time out, all sources of reinforcement are removed. Talking to, maintaining eye contact or providing other forms of attention to the student when placing or removing him/her from time out will reduce the effectiveness of the intervention. Interactions with the student – ideally – should be minimal and emotionally neutral. The time out area should be devoid of all reinforcing stimuli.

As much as possible, time out should be issued immediately following the occurrence of inappropriate behavior. Immediacy is crucial to insuring that the student associates removal from reinforcement with negative behavior. It is also important for staff at that time to give a brief verbal reprimand which clearly specifies the inappropriate behavior. Specifically, this would mean placing the child in time out without a lengthy explanation, but with a brief matter-of-fact description of his or her negative behavior. The duration period for time out can be kept relatively short. Research indicates that one to five minute time out periods are effective in reducing the frequency of inappropriate behavior for most individuals (Kazdin, 1980; White & Barley, 1990). Shorter periods can be selected first and then lengthened if necessary. For safety reasons, the student in a time out area must be monitored during the entire period. In the event that the student engages in self-injurious behavior, time out should be discontinued and an alternative approach implemented. When the time out period ends and the child is ready to be released, it would be important to minimize any secondary gain. This could be accomplished by giving a very brief verbal prompt (e.g., stating the child's name and phrase such as "time in") followed by a directive for the student to correct the behavior that initially led to time out.

Staff must take a proactive approach by explaining the procedure to students prior to implementation. This should include a statement about the conditions leading to time out and behaviors that will end it. In addition to a verbal description, it may also be helpful to display the "rules" of time out and have students actually "practice" taking appropriate time outs during a neutral time.

While there are no definitive governmental regulations that describe physical space requirements for time out rooms, reasonable standards and common decency would suggest that a time out room be large enough to permit safe movement as well as safe entry and exit and not be locked in any way. The room must provide a means to continuously monitor the student, both visually and aurally. A student who is agitated to the point where a time out intervention is required has the potential to harm him/herself, intentionally or unintentionally. The area should have adequate lighting and ventilation and the temperature should be within a normal comfort range. The room should be clean and free of sharp objects and fixtures that could be potentially dangerous to a student. The room must, of course, meet all fire and safety codes.

As any staff member who works with troubled children must understand, it is imperative to be sensitive to the issues of individual children. For example, time out would never be an appropriate intervention for a claustrophobic child, a child who has experienced severe trauma involving imprisonment or a child who has a medical condition that might jeopardize his/her own health. In all instances, physical restraint and isolation time out procedures would be used only as a last resort.

- *Response Cost.* Response cost is a widely used behavioral strategy that involves the removal of previously earned or acquired reinforcers (e.g., tangible or token) contingent upon the occurrence of inappropriate behavior. A number of investigators have reported positive results using response cost to reduce aggressive and disruptive behavior in children and adolescents (Forman, 1980; Kaufman & O'Leary, 1972; Kendall & Braswell, 1985; Salend & Allen, 1985).

Goldstein and Keller (1987) offer some very helpful guidelines for behavior managers to follow when implementing a response cost procedure that involves either token or non-token reinforcement removal. As with positive reinforcement plans, the first step would be to have a clear and behaviorally specific definition of the inappropriate behavior(s) whose occurrence will result in a loss of reinforcers. For example, rather than using a broad term such as "is being aggressive, " it would be more helpful to specify individual behaviors such as "making threats, swearing, giving put-downs, hitting, or pushing others." Next, the behavior manager would need to determine the actual cost that would be incurred contingent upon the display of inappropriate behavior. Although there is no set rule for making this determination, you would probably want to take into consideration such factors as the relation of the points or tokens that could be earned to those that can be lost, the severity of the inappropriate behavior, or whether the cost would be a finite or variable number. Once the costs have been determined, the contingency rule must be clearly communicated to the student(s). Particularly with token systems, it can be helpful to visually display the token, point or privilege value of appropriate and inappropriate behaviors so there will be little chance of misunderstanding. Walker (1979) has also suggested that students be regularly informed of their own earning status. He developed a rather easy to use feedback system that allows students to track their cumulative progress with information that includes: (a) when earnings or costs have been applied, (b) the specific behaviors these were applied to, (c) and how many points have been lost or earned.

As is the case when designing most behavioral plans, the ultimate success of any response cost program will rest upon the creative skills of the behavior manager who must take into consideration a number of motivational factors. In addition, the same general requirements that apply to extinction and time out (i.e., consistent application, immediate delivery, and an impartial and automatic response) also exist for response cost.

The Use of Punishment Methods.   Because of the concern and controversy over the use of punishment, I am somewhat reluctant to include a section on this topic. This is further complicated by the fact that the literature on the effects of punishment provides a mixed review that lends support to both the pro- and anti-punishment positions. For example, research has linked punishment to such negative side effects as counteraggression toward the punisher, withdrawl from social contact, selective avoidance (refraining from negative behavior but only when being watched), modeling of punishing behavior and damage to relationships (Azrin & Holtz, 1966; Bandura, 1973). In contrast, studies that offer support for the use of punishment have shown that it can result in a rapid reduction in negative behavior along with the consequent increase in providing new sources of reinforcement, improved discrimination learning and increased social and emotional behavior (Axelrod & Apache, 1982; Newsom, Favell & Rincover, 1982; Van Houten, 1982).

What most investigators do tend to agree on is the fact that the main effect of punishment is only a temporary suppression of undesirable behavior (Goldstein & Keller, 1987). It is also critical to understand that punishment, like time out and extinction, will not teach an individual how to engage in an alternative and desirable behavior. Consequently, it is imperative that any punishment procedure be used in tandem with teaching and reinforcement procedures in order to increase the likelihood that the individual will engage in more appropriate alternative behaviors.

In the following sections, my discussion of punishment methods refers only to the use of verbal reprimands and overcorrection. Because of both professional and ethical considerations, I am in no way suggesting the use of corporal punishment.

- *Verbal Reprimands.* Verbal reprimands are perhaps one of the most common means used by teachers to correct behavior and there is a good deal of research that supports its use for reducing disruptive behavior (Jones & Miller, 1974), physical aggression (Hall, Exelrod, Foundopoulos, Shellman, Campbell & Cranston, 1971) and other acting out behaviors (O'Leary, Kaufman, Kass & Drabman, 1970). What these and other studies have determined is that reprimands are most effective when (a) they are used consistently following each occurrence of the target behavior; (b) when staff issue the reprimand using a firm voice tone, with good eye contact, close physical proximity and include a clear statement that describes the inappropriate behavior; (c) when it is used early in the behavior chain or series of occurrences; and (d) when it is followed by a statement of praise when the individual corrects his/her behavior (Goldstein & Keller, 1987).

- *Overcorrection.* Overcorrection is an aversive technique that is designed to correct the consequences of an inappropriate behavior (restitution overcorrection) and to encourage the individual to practice more appropriate replacement behavior (positive practice overcorrection) (Foxx & Azrin, 1972). Either component can be used in combination or separately. With restitution, the individual is required to restore a damaged situation to a better condition (i.e., to overcorrect) than when originally encountered. The positive practice component would require the individual to repeatedly practice the correct alternative behavior. For example, a student who overturned chairs or a table when angry might be required to not only pick up the chairs, but also clean them and straighten all chairs and tables in the room. The positive practice would involve requiring the student to sit appropriately at the table for a predetermined time or to practice walking by chairs without kicking them.

    According to the research, restitution and positive practice overcorrection are most effective when they are topographically related to the inappropriate behavior, occur immediately following misbehavior, involve extended duration and active performance by the individual (Foxx & Azrin, 1972; Ollendick & Mattson, 1978). Goldstein and Keller (1987) referred to two overcorrection strategies that have been applied to aggressive behavior. One form, designed for more highly agitated individuals, is Quiet Training (Foxx, Foxx, Jones & Kiely, 1980). Another method, referred to as Social Apology Training (Foxx & Azrin, 1972; Ollendick & Mattson, 1976), has been used with less agitated individuals. With Quiet Training, the person is required to remain quiet and relaxed on a bed or chair until all signs of agitation have been eliminated for a predetermined amount of time. In Social Apology Training, the individual must reassure everyone who was present during the earlier disturbance that the inappropriate behaviors will not reoccur.

Overcorrection has been found effective in helping to reduce various problematic behaviors in child, adolescent and adult populations. For additional information, I would encourage the reader to review earlier studies by Foxx and Azrin (1972), Foxx and Bechtel (1983) and Preator, Peterson, Jenson, and Ashcroft (1984).

Behavioral Contracting

Helping students set goals and contracting can provide very useful guidelines for identifying what students hope to accomplish and the actions they must take to reach their goals. Students with behavioral problems or those who have experienced repeated failure often have difficulty setting realistic goals. In my experience, they tend to set goals that are either too easy or too difficult that results in setting them up for failure. However, when goals are stated in specific and attainable terms, students can begin to take control of their actions.

Contracting is a method used to promote behavior change by specifying target behaviors and contingencies to all who are involved in the change process. It differs from other behavior management strategies in that a contract describes the rewards and responsibilities for *both or all* parties involved who desire behavior change from each other (Wielkiewicz, 1986). Each element of the process should be stated so clearly that they may be written into an agreement that is understandable and acceptable to all parties involved (DeRisi & Butz, 1975). Contracts are to be

developed jointly with the student if they are to be successful.
Terms and conditions should never be imposed.

Basically, as in our everyday adult life, a contract is a
structured means of scheduling the exchange of positive
reinforcement (rewards, positive events) between two or more
persons for fulfilling certain responsibilities. Well written
contracts include the following elements: (1) the task or behavior
to perform; (2) the performance criteria; and (3) the consequence
for fulfillment of that requirement (Connolly et al., 1995).

Knowing where to begin in selecting the target behavior is
not always an easy task. Most certainly, you will need good data
that is specific and reliable (i.e., more than one person should be
able to agree that the behavior did or did not occur). Collecting
data during a baseline period is often helpful for a number of
reasons since you will be able to answer some key questions. Is it
really a problem? If so, how much of a problem is it? What
would be a realistic initial goal to establish? Good data will, of
course, enable you to measure progress or the lack thereof and
make adjustments accordingly.

As others have suggested (Connolly et al., 1995; DeRisi &
Butz, 1975), the first behavior to work on may not necessarily be
the most important because the most important behavior may be
difficult to change if you attempt to focus on it directly. For
example, a student who has a *bad attitude* toward authority and is
quick to argue with adults would obviously be a problem for the
student and adults involved yet this behavior may not be easy to
resolve by focusing on it directly. What may be more helpful
might be to consider behaviors that had previously gone
unrewarded and then try to alter these which might reduce the
frequency of arguing with teachers. At the very least, the target
behavior should be functional in that, if performed more
frequently, it will increase the student's chances of getting rewards
from the natural environment. Helping a student speak to teachers
in a socially acceptable manner, for example, may influence
teachers to be less critical and more likely to reinforce appropriate
behavior in the future (DeRisi & Butz, 1975).

As suggested earlier, target behaviors should be
operationally defined. That is, they must be described in
observable and measureable terms that are easily understood by
all. Behaviors that are clearly defined typically include the

elements of a good news story: who, what, when, where and how (many). The why question should have already been answered when you selected the first behavior to work on. Preferably, the contract should be stated in positive terms. Your performance criteria should also specify to what criteria the task is to be performed (i.e., how well, how long, how often, etc.).

The contract should be reasonable and capable of being achieved by the student. Again, your baseline data will inform you as to how the student is currently performing and what initial goal would be realistic. Remember, it is not unrealistic to consider contracting as a series of negotiated agreements that can gradually shape preferred behaviors over time. In fact, it is unlikely that one contract will be sufficient. It can also be helpful for students to know that the contract is open to renegotiation at any time (Rhode, Jensen & Reavis, 1992). This communicates to the student that you are open to his or her input and sensitive to the student's effort to work toward change.

Determining the consequences that can be earned should, again, involve the student. In doing so, you not only communicate that the child's behavior change efforts are appreciated, but you increase the likelihood of success because children's ideas are frequently more fair, accurate and rewarding to them (Connolly et al., 1995). Consequences should be fairly easily obtainable and neither expensive nor time-consuming. To be effective, they must also be absolutely contingent on the desired behavior and not available through other sources. That is, with the exception of demonstrating the preferred behavior, the student should not have access to the privilege or reward at any other time. Contracts can also contain a bonus clause for exceptional performance and/or a penalty clause that describes sanctions for failing to meet terms of the agreement. Finally, there should be some method of monitoring and evaluating the contract that may involve nothing more than a simple data collection system (e.g., number of points earned or stickers received on a chart). The last clause in a contract should also specify when the contract will be reviewed and renegotiated.

Written contracts come in any number of variations and the specific provisions contained in any contract can be infinite. The exact format is relatively unimportant as long as you include the following elements:

1) The starting, ending and renegotiation dates.
2) Clear and concise definition of the target behavior(s).
3) Amount or type of reward to be delivered.
4) The reward delivery schedule.
5) Signatures of all parties involved.
6) A schedule for reviewing progress.
7) A statement of the bonus or penalty clause (optional). (DeRisi & Butz, 1975).

While using behavior contracts, teachers and clinicians should be aware of the fact that their first efforts may not be successful. Whether we want to accept this or not, behavior change efforts are rarely easy and our long-term commitment to helping students improve their behavior and adjustment is what really counts. Before deciding to scrap everything you've started, it might be helpful to consider some of the following questions:

- Does the student understand the contract process? Is it positive and fair?
- Does the student clearly understand what is required?
- Does the student require specific skill instruction to demonstrate new behavior?
- Does it provide for immediate reinforcement following occurrence of the desired behavior?
- Is the reinforcement frequent and in small amounts?
- Is the student obtaining the reinforcement from another source?
- Is the reinforcement powerful enough?
- Is the task requirement realistic for the student to achieve?
- Are there small approximations to the desired behavior?
- Have the data been verified as accurate?

Behavior contracts can be extremely helpful in working with unmotivated children and youth. They can outline teacher expectations and rules of conduct, academic expectations, and consequences for any number of desired or undesired behaviors. The key is to involve the student, start at his or her current performance level and shape behavior to the desired goal in a systematic manner over time. A sample behavioral contract is provided in Figure 2.

Figure 2 - Sample Behavioral Contract

BEHAVIOR CONTRACT

Effective Dates: From Oct. 2   **To** Oct. 13
Review Date: Oct. 13
  We, the undersigned, agree to perform the following behaviors:

If Dan uses his "keep calm"   **then** he will be given
Strategy when prompted by   immediate praise and
an adult during recess,   50 points to be added to
          his classroom "savings"
          account.

Bonus: If Dan uses his "keep calm" strategy without being cued or prompted by an adult during recess, he will earn 100 bonus points. All points can be redeemable at the class store each Friday.

If Dan does not need to use his "keep calm" strategy at all, he will also earn 100 bonus points each day.

Penalty: none

Signed_____
          _____
          _____

PROGRESS RECORD

10/2	10/3	10/4	10/5	10/6	
yes	-	yes	yes	-	
BF	BF	BF	GD	BF	(teacher initials)

Self-Management Strategies

Undoubtedly, one of the most ubiquitous goals in education is to teach children to control their own actions. Robert Gagne (1965), a leading educational psychologist, once stated that the ultimate goal of education is to progressively wean students from dependence upon teachers and teach them to do what is necessary to guide their own behavior – in other words, to teach themselves. One could easily argue that teaching children to control their own behavior is educationally more efficient and pragmatic in that it enables the teacher to devote more time to teaching and less time to classroom mechanics and behavior management. Teaching self-control may not only decrease the demand for direct intervention by teachers but also improve the maintenance of treatment effects (McLaughlin, 1976) and increase the chances of transfer of treatment effects (e.g., Neilans & Isreal, 1981). As Workman and Hector (1978) have noted, self-management strategies can be used to address any number of student behaviors including on-task behavior, disruptive behavior and academic product behaviors.

Models of self-control differ along many dimensions. For example, Kanfer's model (1970) of self-control involves self-monitoring (self-observation), self-evaluation (comparison of one's observation with another standard) and self-reinforcement. Meichenbaum and Goodman (1971) were among the first researchers to examine self-instruction strategies in helping impulsive and hyperactive children improve their academic and social performance. Essentially, children were taught to talk to themselves appropriately in order to guide their behavior and evaluate their own performance. Blackwood (1970) developed a procedure similar to self-instruction that he labeled verbal mediation training. With this procedure, students are asked to copy essays that teach them to assess their own behavior and understand the consequences of inappropriate behavior. Each of these dimensions will be described briefly in the following sections.

Self-Monitoring. Self-monitoring has been particularly useful as an intervention strategy because of the reactive effects of observing one's own behavior. While it was initially used as a method of collecting data, clinicians soon learned that when people observed their own behavior, it often caused changes in the behavior. Consequently, many practitioners have taken advantage of the reactive effects of self-monitoring in order to change student behavior (Gardner & Cole, 1988; Mace & Kratochwill, 1988). Self-monitoring is usually successful with children over the age of 8 years and with differing abilities at either the elementary, middle school or high school level. There are basically two tasks involved in any self-monitoring procedure: (1) observation of the behavior itself and (2) recording of observational data. One of the most common methods involves frequency self-monitoring whereby the student would record each behavior as it occurs. Behaviors counted might include the number of times a student talks out in class without permission, or the number of times the student makes an inappropriate noise. Desirable behaviors could also be counted such as the number of math problems completed during class or the number of times a student raises his or her hand for teacher assistance. Frequency self-monitoring is most appropriate for use with behaviors that are discrete (i.e., have a definite beginning and end) and tend to occur often. With this procedure, students can be easily taught to use a simple paper and pencil device to record their tallies such as an index card that might be placed on their desk or a countoon that can serve as a visual reminder to observe behavior.

Countoons (originally developed by Kunzelmann, Cohen, Hulten, Martin & Mingo, 1970) are cartoon versions of recording strategies designed for young children and nonreaders to help them monitor and change their own behaviors. They are relatively simple to construct and typically provide a representation of a student's appropriate and inappropriate behavior, a contingency for meeting criteria and counting frames for recording data. The child could be asked to count the number of times he or she engages in the appropriate behavior, inappropriate behavior or both. If the child reaches a certain criterion, he earns the agreed upon consequence. Figure 3 provides an example of a countoon used to increase hand-raising and reduce impulse shouting out. In this example, if the child keeps his count under a predetermined maximum, he will be able to play basketball.

Figure 3 - Countoon for Hand-Raising to Gain Teacher Attention

What I do		
Raise my hand	Shout out	Raise my hand
	1 2 3 4 5 6 7 8 9 10 11 12 13 14 15	

What Happens
Play basketball

Practically any behavior that can be defined and reduced to a simple cartoon frame is appropriate for a countoon. Students with disabilities have used such devices to make positive changes with respect to aggressive behavior (Gumpel & Shlomit, 2000), and social behaviors including attention-to-task, peer interactions and cooperative behavior (McDougall, 1998). In addition to inappropriate classroom behavior, teachers can also use countoons to help students with their academic skills (e.g., the number of math problems completed, the number of problems attempted before requesting assistance, vocabulary and sight words recognized within 2 seconds). There are a number of ways to adapt countoons to meet the needs of specific students. For example, the child could use smiley faces and straight faces instead of numbers for counting if the child cannot count. The counting frames could also contain other symbols that the child might associate with appropriate behavior (e.g., stars, stickers) or the child could draw his or her own pictures that depict the behaviors to be recorded.

Some excellent and helpful information on general methods and applications of self-monitoring to school problems can be found in references by Workman (1982), Bloomquist (1996),Lloyd, Landrum and Hallahan (1991),Daly and Ranalli (2003), Gumpel & Shlomit (2000), McDougall & Brady (1998) and McDougall (1998).

Self-Evaluation. Self-evaluation or self-rating is another practical procedure used to modify student behavior. It is best suited for continuous behaviors such as on-task behavior, direction following, listening, focusing, participating, etc. As with self-monitoring, the first step would be to decide exactly what specific behavior you wish to change and in what setting you want to change it. It is critical that the student clearly understands what the appropriate behavior is and looks like. In many cases it can be helpful to model these behaviors for the student. After selecting a target behavior, you would devise a rating system or scale (e.g., 0 to 5 or 0 to 2) that gives a clear definition of what each rating means. Your next step would be to decide upon the time interval during which ratings would occur. It is often helpful to keep time intervals short (e.g., 5, 10, or 30 minutes) especially with younger children although manageability must also be considered. As student behavior improves, it may be possible to gradually increase the time interval. The next step in designing a self-evaluation intervention is to determine the mechanics of the system (i.e., exactly how will the students rate themselves?). The final step is to implement the management procedure by having students practice giving themselves ratings while providing them with corrective feedback.

Over the years I have used self-ratings as a treatment technique in a number of my own groups. For example, in a social skills group involving 8 to 10 year old boys, I selected compliance with group rules as my target behavior. The rating system ranged from zero to five with the following performance criteria:

> 5 = Excellent: Followed all group rules; no verbal warnings; 100% participation.
> 4 = Very Good: Minor infraction of rules (e.g., interrupting others); accepted criticism, 90% participation.
> 3 = Average: Followed group rules approximately 80% of time; given three reminders to correct behavior; no serious offenses.
> 2 = Below Average: Followed group rules approximately 60% to 80% of the time; broke one or more rules to extent that behavior was not acceptable.
> 1 = Poor: Broke one or more rules for more than half of the period or engaged in a higher degree of inappropriate behavior.
> 0 = Unacceptable: Unable to follow any rules; left group.

To start, we collected data during a baseline phase (5 – 10 days) that helped establish the criteria for reinforcement. In phase two – external reinforcement - student ratings were issued by the adult group leader using the 0 to 5 point scale. Ratings converted to points that students could later spend for a variety of rewards. Once students were able to meet behavioral expectations fairly consistently, they would move to the match phase where both student and staff rate independently on the 0 to 5- point scale. Points would then be awarded as follows: 1. Student within one point = keeps points he/she gave to him/herself; 2. Student has an exact match = keeps points plus one bonus point; 3. Student is off by more than one point = no points awarded for that time interval. As students became more accurate in their own ratings (i.e., they had many matched ratings), they would proceed to the final phase of self-rating. At this point, students would simply be asked to give themselves a rating based on perceptions of their own performance and would record this on their point sheet. On occasion, we would do a random "match" rating in order to help maintain the honesty factor in student ratings.

What I find useful about this strategy is that it is not only efficient, but can be very individualized and flexible as it helps kids increase ownership and awareness of their own behavior. For example, in my groups, kids will move at their own rate of progress in either an up or down fashion based on their performance. Determining criteria for moving from one phase to another is strictly up to the adult as there are no hard and fast rules. Probably as a minimum, you might want to maintain a student on any phase for 5 to 10 days, but again, it will depend on your population and unique circumstance. To fade this system while maintaining the use of self-ratings, it would be easiest to extend the rating intervals, extend the time between reinforcement or both.

Self-Reinforcement. Often included under the umbrella of self-control along with self-assessment, self-recording and self-evaluation is self-reinforcement. Essentially, with this technique, students must be able to determine whether their performance on a task meets criteria before presenting themselves with actual reinforcers which may involve anything from statements of self-praise to access to desirable objects or activities. In his text, *Teaching behavioral self-control to students,* Workman (1982) described basic methods of using overt self-reinforcement to help students improve on-task and academic product behaviors and reduce disruptive behavior. Workman maintained that an initial step in implementing any self-reinforcement program is to have students self-monitor and record their own behavior using either frequency or interval monitoring. This only stands to reason since students must, of course, determine whether they have engaged in the target behavior that will lead to reinforcement. In many cases, student recordings are converted to points or tokens that can then be redeemed for objects or activities that the student finds desirable. For example, in a simple group management system, students could earn additional free time as a reinforcement activity contingent upon a certain number of points they received based on their own self-recordings. Students who do not earn sufficient points would not be eligible for extra recess or free time.

With any intervention using self-reinforcement as a component, the child must have the necessary skills and understanding of the steps toward performing the target behavior. In addition, three criteria must also be satisfied before self-reinforcement can occur: (1) The performance standard must be adopted that establishes the quantity or quality of the target behavior required for self-reinforcement; (2) The reinforcement must be delivered on a conditional basis; and (3) The child must have control over the desired reinforcers.

Another technique related to self-reinforcement is goal setting. This can be a very helpful technique since students with significant behavioral problems often have difficulty setting realistic goals (Sprick, Sprick & Garrison, 1993). They tend to either select goals that are too easy which produces little sense of accomplishment, or too difficult which then sets them up for failure. Indeed, many of these students have difficulty with direction and purpose. They may want to "be successful" or realize they need to "try harder," but fail to understand what is necessary to develop the skills and habits that are essential for success.

With goal setting, students not only learn to establish plans for themselves but also establish the criteria for success. Goal setting provides a course of action that can help students identify what they hope to accomplish and the specific steps they can take to reach their goals. This process may help students increase their motivation to change and may often be most effective when combined with other behavioral interventions including contracting and self-monitoring. Ideally, what is also needed is ongoing adult support in the form of regular progress monitoring and the identification of ways that adults might be able to help the student reach his or her goal(s).

Self-Instruction. Student directed self-instruction has been a strategy used to address a number of problems including academic performance (Gettinger, 1985; Fish & Mendola, 1981986; Whitman & Johnson, 1983), impulsivity (Graybill, Jamison & Swedlik, 1984; Kendall & Braswell, 1985), disruptive behavior (Coats, 1979), negative attitudes (Sprick, Sprick & Garrison, 1993) and anger management (Bloomquist, 1996). Essentially, self-instruction training or "self-talk" involves teaching students to use covert verbalizations to guide their overt behavior. Many clinicians have utilized Meichenbaum and Goodman's model, as described in their 1971 article entitled, "Training impulsive children to talk to themselves: A means of developing self-control" (Meichenbaum & Goodman, 1971). The method involves five steps: (1) the adult models the self-instruction out loud while performing the task; (2) the student performs the task while following the adult's self-instruction; (3) the student self-instructs while doing the task; (4) the student performs the task while whispering the self-instruction; (5) the student self-instructs silently.

Teaching students to use coping self-talk strategies or restructuring their self-talk have been very appropriate interventions to help children overcome negative thoughts about themselves and to maintain self-control when angry or frustrated. For example, it would be important to explain to a child that self-talk involves saying helpful things to oneself (i.e., helpful thoughts) in order to stay calm and in control. The child would then be encouraged to think of words or phrases that could be helpful as reminders to stay calm such as the following:

- "Chill out."   - "Keep cool. I can handle this."
- "Relax."   - "Don't lose it."
- "Take some deep breaths."
- "Take it easy. It will be okay."

Typically, this intervention would need to be paired with other interventions that would most likely involve specific skills training (i.e., modeling and role-playing), monitoring of student performance, relaxation strategies and reinforcement procedures. A good place to begin would be to demonstrate for the child the use of coping self-talk when you might be angry or frustrated. After several trials, the child could then practice appropriate use of this strategy via role plays while using his or her own coping self-statements. To encourage practice in real-life settings, it might then be appropriate to implement a more formal program in which the child would be asked to keep a log of those events related to his or her upset feelings with information including what the trigger or causal event was, what angry signals he noticed (e.g., body, thinking, action signals), what he or she did to cope with the situation and how he or she would rate oneself in terms of how well they were able to cope. Bloomquist (1996) has developed a very practical guide and worksheet designed for both children and parents that can be used to structure this type of anger-coping process.

Sprick, Sprick and Garrison (1993) have also developed a

step-by-step intervention to help students use self-talk to their advantage. They begin by reviewing with the student the nature and scope of the problem as well as the overall goal(s). For example, does the student display self-control problems, engage in excessive self-blame, or display a negative attitude characterized by excessive criticism of others? What is important for the child to understand is that what we say to ourselves is related to both self-perception and behavior. What Sprick et al. (1993) emphasize is that when we succeed at something, we tend to feel good about ourselves and when we think in positive terms, we tend to behave in more positive ways. In contrast, if we think negatively, it is more likely that we will have difficulty being successful with the task at hand or in our interactions with others.

Once the scope of the problem is defined, the student is asked to list the types of negative statements he or she makes in various situations. Other adults can also supply examples of such statements. This is important because, in many instances, negative self-talk is habitual and beyond the awareness level of the student and it can be used to help the student understand how negative statements interfere with his goal. After various negative statements have been identified, the student would be encouraged to replace these negative thoughts with more positive or alternative ones. For example, an alternative statement could be used to replace the following negative statement:

Negative: "I'm stupid. I'm always messing up!"
Alternative: "It's okay to make a mistake. Everyone
          does."

Again, because such negative self-talk is likely to be habitual, it would be important to have several examples of positive self-talk for the student to see as appropriate replacement statements. The authors also emphasize the need for adult support in order prompt the student to make positive statements, particularly in specific or difficult situations. The student would identify a specific "signal" (e.g., raising an eyebrow, thumbs up gesture, etc.) that the adult would then use to prompt the student to make a positive or coping statement. Again, because negative self-talk may be deeply ingrained, it would be important to review student progress regularly and allow for continued practice of the skill. In certain cases, it may also be helpful to utilize a self-monitoring procedure where the student records or counts his own negative and positive statements. With this type of intervention, the student could be directed to make a positive statement whenever he records a negative statement. Sprick et al. (1993) provide various self-monitoring forms that can be used for this type of intervention.

Verbal Mediation. Another class of interventions, somewhat similar to self-instruction training, has been based on the use of verbal mediation - the process of talking to oneself to guide problem solving. Often referred to as cognitive problem-solving interventions, these methods have been effective in improving self-control (Dupper & Krishef, 1993; Feindler, Marriott & Iwata, 1984), social skills (Knoff, 2002) and decreasing verbal aggression (Schlichter & Horan, 1981) and physical aggression in children (Guerra & Slaby, 1990: Lochman, Burch, Curry & Lampron, 1984). Cognitive problem-solving interventions typically involve training children to engage in a series of steps that can then guide them as they cope with problematic situations. For example, *Cognitive Mediation Training* (Guerra & Slaby, 1990) focuses on teaching children the following eight steps when problem-solving:

1. Is there a problem?
2. Stop and think.
3. Why is there a conflict?
4. What do I want?
5. Think of solutions.
6. Look at consequences.
7. Choose what to do and do it.
8. Evaluate results.

Project ACHIEVE's *Stop and Think Social Skills Program* (Knoff, 2002) is another excellent approach that involves language mediation training when teaching, reinforcing or using any social skill. Specifically, the program uses a five-step language sequence that includes the following:

- "Stop and Think!"
- "Are you going to make a Good Choice or Bad Choice?"
- "What are your Choices or Steps?"
- "Just Do It!"
- "Good Job!"

The *Stop and Think!* step reminds students to slow down and think about how they want to deal with the situation. The *Good or Bad Choice* step serves to help students focus on what kind of choice they want to make which may include adult reminders of what positive and negative consequences would occur. The *What are your Choices?* step helps students think of a specific plan of action before attempting to solve the problem. It is at this point that students are instructed in the specific steps needed for the skill they have focused on. As with most social skills training models, students would first be taught the individual steps of the social skill. Demonstration or modeling of the skill by an adult could then occur with follow-up opportunities for role-playing and extended practice during the day. The *Just Do It!* step would prompt students to carry out their plan and evaluate whether or not it worked. Finally, the *Good Job!* step would serve to remind students to reinforce themselves for using a social skill and making a good choice (Knoff, 2000, 2002).

The development of a number of these cognitive problem-solving or verbal mediation interventions have their origin stemming from the work of Luria (1961) and Vygotsky (1962). These Russian psychologists noted that language provides both a social and instrumental function from an early age and, as the child develops, can serve as an internal regulator of behavior. Luria (1961), for example, conceptualized stages in the development of verbal control over behavior as progressing from a child's ability to respond to external inhibitory commands (e.g., parents) to overt self-talk and, finally, covert self-talk. Specifically, in the second year of life a majority of children start to respond to inhibitory parental commands but do not respond to their own overt inhibitory statements. As they mature into the preschool years, they begin to regulate their own behavior in response to overt verbalizations although covert commands do not typically have any regulatory effect. Somewhere between ages five to seven, children then begin to develop the capacity to inhibit or regulate their behavior through covert verbal activity (e.g., private speech or whispering) (Meichenbaum & Goodman, 1969).

In relation to this earlier work, investigators have associated deficits in the development and use of verbal mediation processes in children with academic and social-behavioral problems (Camp, 1977; Gordon, 1979). In particular, children with impulse control problems, hyperactivity and aggressive behaviors have been the focus of much attention and there have been a number of interventions developed to help increase their verbal mediation activity. Examples of such programs include Lochman's *Anger Coping* (Lochman & Lenhart, 1993), Schlicter and Horan's (1981) *Stress Inoculation*, the *Coping Power* program (Lochman & Wells, 1996) and Camp and Bash's (1981) *Think Aloud* program.

Verbal mediation essays represent another approach used with students to help them think about (mediate) their inappropriate behavior while also serving as an aversive consequence (Blackwood, 1970; Dowd, Tobias, Connolly, Criste & Nelson, 1993). With this strategy, students either copy essays or write essays in response to questions about their behavior and the consequences of their behavior. If a student misbehaves, for example, he or she would be given an essay to copy or answer that relates directly to the behavior the teacher wants to reduce (e.g., one for talking out, one for swearing, one for hitting others, etc.). In an earlier study involving highly disruptive eighth and ninth grade students, Blackwood (1970) reported significant decreases in disruptive incidents per class session using verbal mediation essays. Students who were given unrelated essays demonstrated no changes in behavior. Similarly, MacPherson, Candee and Hohman (1974) reported positive results using mediation essays to eliminate disruptive lunchroom behavior with elementary age students in grades one through six.

Verbal mediation essays typically contain some variation of the following four questions and answers: (1) "What did I do wrong?"; (2) "Why is that wrong?"; (3) "What should I do instead?"; (4) "What good things could happen to me?" In response to each question is a brief paragraph that provides a specific answer. The vocabulary level would be appropriate for the age of the student. The following is an example of what this might look like in response to a problem of leaving the area of supervision:

BEHAVIOR ESSAY
(Leaving the Area of Supervision)

1.   **What Did I Do Wrong?** I got into trouble for leaving the room without permission. This is one of our class rules that I broke. Now I have to write this essay to help me learn that it is not okay to leave the area of supervision without permission.

2.   **Why is That Wrong?** It is wrong to leave any class without permission. It shows that I do not have respect for rules and it can be disruptive for others. Adults will have to spend extra time correcting my behavior. If my parent(s) finds out that I am not being responsible at school, they may not let me do some of the things I want at home.

3.   **What Should I Do?** What I should do from now on is ask permission to leave the class. If my teachers don't give me permission, I should accept "no", stay calm and just stay in class without arguing. I can say to myself, "I can follow the rules." When I want to leave the room I will wait to get permission first.

4.   **What Good Things Might Happen to Me?** When I follow the class rules, other people will see me as a responsible person. I won't get into trouble or lose points. My teachers will be more likely to let me leave without a hassle if I ask them first for permission. My parents may hear that I have been doing a good job following rules and might give me more privileges at home because they think I can handle it.

Before I leave the class, I will get permission.

Student signature_____ Date_____

      When using mediation essays, it may be appropriate and, at times, necessary to modify the method, criteria or format. For example, the simplest method would be to provide an example for the student to copy. However, one could also take dictation from the student or have the student develop his or her own essay in response to the formatted questions. Criteria might involve completion of an essay or completion to a specified percentage of accuracy (e.g., spelling, mechanics, neatness). Depending upon the nature of the problem, the format could also be extended to include a written apology that contains a statement of remorse and description of the appropriate behavior as well as a desire to return to the program or classroom (Dowd, et. al, 1993).

SUMMARY

For many students with significant behavioral problems, individual management plans are needed. Such plans should not focus exclusively on simply decreasing behaviors but also on increasing more positive, replacement behaviors that can improve the individual's quality of life. Ideally, the design and selection of individual behavior plans can occur through a collaborative process involving staff who work directly with the student together with parents and the behavioral consultant. Not only can this create an improved sense of ownership for those who will be implementing the plan but also help to insure that the intervention will be seen as acceptable and implemented as intended.

To avoid the "consult and hope" approach that school practitioners may use when consulting with teachers, Gresham (1989) suggested that plans remain as simple as possible, that plans be put in writing and that teachers receive training and support in order to implement the intervention as designed. Stages in plan development were described beginning with the initial referral concern(s), followed by data collection, problem analysis, development of the written plan, implementation, evaluation and follow-up.

A range of individual strategies were also described including basic contingency management methods, behavioral contracts, and self-management interventions.

CHAPTER 6

GROUP BEHAVIOR MANAGEMENT

ESSENTIAL ELEMENTS

There are many group management systems in existence designed to promote positive behaviors and reduce inappropriate actions. While there may be no simple formula for designing the perfect system, there are certain elements that researchers and practitioners have found to be essential in terms of achieving success (Brooks, 2001; Council for Exceptional Children-*Research Connections*, 1997; Dowd et al., 1993; Duke, 1989; Peterson, 1998; Gaustad, 1992). The components of successful group behavior management systems can probably best be reduced to the following:

1. *A set of beliefs about what behaviors, attitudes and relationships are valued.* School personnel should be very clear on what behaviors and relationships they wish to promote in their setting.

2. *A commitment to developing strong student-teacher relationships.*
   The development of positive student-teacher relationships is especially critical for children who enter the classroom with many unmet needs and behaviors that interfere with their social adjustment and academic achievement. While a positive relationship will not resolve all problems, it can certainly go a long way in terms of positively influencing student behavior (Jones & Jones, 1990). Effective classrooms typically consist of a combination of warmth and caring along with an appropriate amount of firmness, tolerance and competent teaching (Shores, Gunter & Jack, 1993; Steinberg, 1992).

3. *A set of clearly defined behavioral expectations.* Whether you are developing a classroom or program-wide management plan, it will be essential to establish a clear

list of rules that set the standard for student behavior. A list of rules need not be extensive. A good rule of thumb is to establish only three to five rules that can then serve as guidelines for student behavior. Rules should encourage behavior that optimizes learning for all and should be stated in positive terms. In this regard, students are reminded of what they should be doing rather than what they shouldn't. Examples of positively stated rules include:

- Follow directions
- Arrive on time and with all materials
- Stay focused on your work
- Cooperate with others
- Raise your hand for help
- Keep feet and hands to yourself
- Be respectful of others

In many cases it may be appropriate to develop rules with student input. This can be helpful in getting students to take greater ownership of the rules that will guide their behavior. Rationales that relate to each of the rules should also be provided in order to help students recognize and understand how they and others will benefit from having such behavioral guidelines. Once selected, some form of public posting of rules should occur. This will then serve as the focus of your behavior management efforts. Whether you are reinforcing responsible behavior or correcting inappropriate behavior, students can be told how their behavior relates to the rules.

4. *A Programmatic effort to help students learn and develop skills related to self-control, problem solving, conflict resolution and social relationships.* Meaningful and lasting behavior change will not occur if the focus is strictly on establishing control and issuing consequences. Rather, there must be a strong teaching component that addresses those important social and behavioral skills that many students lack. Similarly, programs should take on a very proactive approach in teaching students how to deal successfully in a variety of routine situations (e.g.,

transition time, group activities and rituals, cafeteria behavior, support or crisis room behavior, etc.).

5. *A set of well-defined consequences for engaging in positive and negative behavior.* Along with a clear understanding of the rules, students must also be informed in advance of the consequences for positive and negative behavior. The behavior management system must contain procedures that students understand and have consequences that are clear and fair. Ideally, appropriate behavior can result in both social as well as other tangible rewards involving privileges, activities or access to preferred items. Consequences for negative behavior might range from simple planned ignoring to verbal reprimand and positive practice or, in cases of severely disruptive behavior, loss of privileges, time out, physical restraint or suspension. All plans should specify a series of consequences that can be used in response to mild to severe forms of disruptive behavior. Whenever possible, consequences should also have some logical connection with the inappropriate behavior.

6. *A dynamic instructional program that engages students in meaningful learning activities.* It should be evident that when students are motivated and involved, their energies are more likely to be focused on the task at hand. One of the best ways to reduce inappropriate behavior is to have a meaningful and authentic instructional program appropriate to student needs.

STEPS IN DEVELOPING GROUP BEHAVIOR MANAGEMENT PLANS

The process of developing any group management plan will, for the most part, be similar to the process used in the design of individual plans that has been discussed earlier. Ideally, this should be a collaborative process that involves all relevant stakeholders including staff, students (as appropriate) and parents. As a starting point, there must be a clear understanding of behavioral goals for your students. Of course, if specific behaviors are not currently in a student's repertoire, then lessons would need to be designed to teach that student the appropriate behavior(s).

Once specific behavioral goals have been identified, you would then design a management system that provides the students with reinforcers for successfully meeting behavioral objectives. Initial tasks would most likely involve the following:

- Determine a method for monitoring behavior and recording points.
- Identify a menu of possible rewards, privileges.
- Establish your economy (i.e., determine point values for each reward).

There are a number of ways of monitoring student behavior and keeping track of points, tokens, plus and minus signs, and so forth. The best monitoring systems are relatively simple, easy to use and age-appropriate. For example, how successfully your students are following class rules may be monitored by recording either a plus or minus sign for specific time intervals as shown in Figure 4.

Figure 4 - Daily Point Record

Name Erica				Week: 1/18	
Time	M	T	W	Th	F
8:00 – 10:30	+				
10:30 – 12:00	--				
12:00 – 1:30	+				
1:30 – 3:00	+				
Number of points	3				

Another method might be to use a predetermined rating scale in which the students receive a variable number of points based on the degree to which they engage in appropriate behavior. This can be especially helpful when behavior needs to improve in quality or across a number of dimensions. For example, students might receive points based on how well they are able to make good transitions: 3 (excellent) = Successful transition independently, 2 (good) = Needed only one reminder or prompt to be successful, 1 (fair) = Needed more than one reminder, or 0 (poor) = Not at all. In this example, a monitoring system that tracks specific time intervals during the day (similar to Figure 4.) may be most useful. Points could simply be added to obtain a daily point total that could then be recorded in a separate log (e.g., a student account book) and maintained by the teacher.

Another key step is to identify a menu of possible rewards and privileges that would be tailored to the interests of the students. It is often best to simply observe what they prefer to do on their own. I also encourage staff to seek student input. This not only provides staff with ideas but also increases student motivation and student investment in the process. Anything the student appears to enjoy is potentially a reinforcer. Try to think of rewards or activities that can be earned quickly as well as those that might take longer to obtain. Tangible rewards should not be the only choice. Privileges and responsibilities are often more powerful than things. Although the list is endless, some possible ideas may include:

- Ten minutes of additional free time.
- Teaching a younger student.
- Working with the custodian.
- Earning additional computer time.
- A free pass to be excused from homework.
- Making brownies in the school kitchen.
- Extra gym.

When assigning points to each reinforcer, you will need to consider a number of factors: 1) the value of the reinforcer in terms of cost and/or adult time required, 2) the monitoring system scale and range of points possible, 3) the amount of time and effort required of the students, and 4) the sophistication of the students. Particularly in the beginning phases of an intervention, rewards and privileges should be quickly earned because, in many cases, it may be unrealistic to expect students to make large and immediate changes in their behavior. When presented with an explanation of the system, the student should be thinking, "I can do this."

When designing a structured reinforcement system, it is often wise to avoid placing any time limits on what the student must do to earn reinforcement. In contrast, allowing students to accumulate points over time is likely to be more effective. For example, systems that require a certain number of points by the end of the day or week have inherent weaknesses and tend to be inflexible. If a student must earn 10 points in a day to receive a reinforcer but earns only 9 and must start over the next day, he or she will very likely become discouraged. Similarly, if the student starts out unsuccessfully, he or she may realize that no matter how well he/she does for the rest of the day, success is not possible. As Sprick, et al. (1993) have discussed, reinforcement systems should have some "forgiveness" built in. In other words, a bad day or a bad hour should not necessarily eclipse a student's effort, negate previous effort or eliminate reinforcement for any future effort.

In addition to the design of reinforcement procedures, you will also need to determine your response to misbehavior. Generally speaking, there are four basic ways to respond to negative behavior: 1) to ignore it, 2) to provide corrective feedback 3) to implement a classroom consequence, or 4) to implement an out-of-class consequence (Sprick et al., 1993). If the behavior does not interfere with teaching and learning, it may be most appropriate to simply ignore it. If the student is either unaware of the misbehavior, does not know that it is inappropriate or lacks a particular skill, then corrective feedback is needed. However, if the misbehavior cannot be ignored, it would probably make sense to issue some type of mild in-class consequence (e.g., time out, loss of free time, etc.). Severe negative behavior involving physical acting out, assault or extreme insubordination would more likely require some form of out-of-class intervention that has been arranged in advance.

Before actual implementation of any system, put the plan in writing and try to anticipate any possible glitches. Mentally rehearsing how the system will work is always helpful. At this point it is also important to determine how to measure the effectiveness of the system. Often this is accomplished by examining your monitoring system since this can provide an ongoing record of student progress. Understand also that the system will need periodic adjustment. As mentioned earlier, your system may initially be designed to allow students to experience easy success. However, as progress is made, the criteria for earning reinforcers may be adjusted. Similarly, the reinforcers may need to be changed or adjusted to reflect more natural reinforcers (e.g., moving the student from tangibles to taking pride in success via student awards). Behavioral expectations and student-specific target behaviors will also be likely to change as student progress occurs.

The final step prior to implementation is to review the system with the students and let them know the intervention is being initiated. Particularly with older students, you would want to engage them as much as possible in helping plan the system. Consequently, this final step would serve as a review and help prepare students for what specifically will be expected. A class meeting format is well suited for this purpose. Students should not only understand the management system, but also the goals and benefits they and others can receive.

STRUCTURED REINFORCEMENT SYSTEMS

Group-oriented structured reinforcement systems are typically used to motivate students to improve their behavior through the use of external rewards. Structured reinforcement systems can take many forms (e.g., token economies, point systems, star charts, level systems) and are well suited for addressing any number of academic and social or behavioral problems. Although such systems are highly intrusive, they are also needed to assist children and youth with severe social-emotional disabilities whose problems have been resistant to simpler solutions. Students who have experienced a lifetime of chaotic, abusive, neglectful, under-supervised or otherwise disruptive home environments and learning histories, are not likely to break deeply ingrained cycles of negative behavior without external supports and rewards. Unlike many students in regular education settings, this population is less likely to be motivated to do their best, less optimistic about the future, less socially skillful and, for some, more likely to seek negative attention. External reinforcement systems can serve to jump start students to improve academic performance and engage in more socially acceptable behavior. This assumes that the student already knows how to exhibit the desired behavior. If not, the plan must include a method to teach the student the desired behavior. Ultimately, external reinforcement systems can and should be viewed as a temporary intervention that can be faded out once students are moving in more positive directions. The following sections offer examples of various structured reinforcement systems that have been proven helpful in reducing disruptive behavior problems in students with severe emotional disturbance.

Behavioral Level Systems

Behavioral level systems, in their simplest form, use points to indicate how a student is performing and determine what privileges that student may receive. Level systems are most appropriate for students needing a high degree of structure, immediate feedback regarding their behavior and short-term consequences. Level systems recognize that varying degrees of structure are needed by different students. Differences in amount of structure are, in most cases, determined by the students' own behavioral performance and acquisition of critical social skills. In most systems, points or token economies are used instead of direct access to privileges for a number of practical reasons. Points allow for immediacy, which is important for students who are at a beginning stage of acquiring new skills. Points also provide greater flexibility in determining the size of the reinforcer. In addition, points avoid problems with satiation.

The Boys Town Model. One of the most comprehensive motivation (level) systems in existence is one that has been developed and used extensively at Father Flanagan's Boys' Home in Boys Town, Nebraska (Father Flanagan's Boys' Home, 1999). In the context of a teaching interaction, student behavior is directly confronted and results in consequences in the form of points. Consequences (points) are issued immediately which helps create increased motivation for change. Students can then use their points to purchase a variety of reinforcers including tangibles, privileges or activities.

The Boys Town model involves three levels that students move through as they develop new skills – Daily Points, Progress and Merit levels. All students begin at the Daily Points level that focuses on the acquisition of skills (i.e., target behavior skills) that are included in the life skills curriculum used at Boys Town (Dowd & Tierney, 1992). Examples of such skills include following directions, accepting criticism or a consequence, getting the teacher's attention, accepting "no" for an answer and resisting peer pressure. At this beginning level, there is a high degree of supervision and frequent feedback regarding behavior as well as immediate consequences and restricted privileges. Staff is expected to engage in 25 to 30 interactions per student each day to help ensure that students are provided sufficient instruction and practice of newly introduced skills. Students carry with them throughout the day a detailed point sheet that serves as a record for both academic and social-behavioral performance. Points generally range from 15,000 to 30,000 daily. Points are earned and recorded immediately for class participation, assignment completion and demonstration of positive social behaviors pertaining to adult and peer relations, classroom behaviors and school rules. Inappropriate behavior results in an immediate awarding of point penalties that are also indicated on the student's point sheet. Students can, however, earn up to half of their points back if they are able to engage in positive practice or correction that involves practice to criteria of a desired response. At the end of each day, students meet individually with a key staff member to review and summarize their behavior, discuss progress towards goals, total and record points earned, guide purchasing from the reward menu and prepare a new card for the next day.

As students begin to develop greater fluency in their use of skills and save a specified number of points necessary to purchase "bonds", they can advance to Progress Level. One bond costs 6,000 points and students must purchase 100 bonds to advance to Progress level. At this level, a majority of basic skills are in place and new target skills are identified. Early on at this second level, 25 to 30 student-staff social interactions (i.e., teaching interactions) continue to occur although this number is gradually faded to 6 to 10 positive social interactions per day. In addition, some of the highly structured and detailed aspects of the Daily Point level are faded. For example, students no longer use a Daily Points card but a Progress card that is much simpler in format with staff ratings given in the form of positive/negative markings rather than points.

The Progress level also differs from the Daily Points level in that students now must negotiate points based on their total positive and negative marks as indicated on their card. This process of negotiation occurs during the student-teacher conference held at the end of the day during which time the rating (e.g., excellent, good, fair, in need of improvement) and point range are determined. For example, an "Excellent" rating would have a point range of 39,000 to 40,000 points and the criteria would involve no negatives (negative marks) for the day.

Conversely, an "In need of Improvement" rating would have a point range of 0 to 24,900 points and the criteria would include two or more major negative marks. Note that higher point ranges are available at this level and students have an opportunity to obtain more privileges. Once the point total is negotiated for the day, points are then written on the Progress card and initialed by student and teacher. The use of points for purchasing while on the Progress level remains the same as the Daily Points level.

Students are able to advance to the highest system level – Merit level – only after purchasing another 100 bonds at 6,000 points each. Students must have no significant behavior problems such as an office referral, time out or safe room use for 10 days just prior to moving up. They must also complete an application and community service project. Service projects are generally determined by each program and involve some form of service to others including peers, teachers, the school or community. Examples might include helping in the lunchroom, tutoring peers, giving school tours for guests or working on a school beautification project. To formalize this process, the Boy's Town model requires students to complete an application for advancement to the Merit level which is then reviewed and approved by a Merit review committee. Upon completion of the Merit application process, students sign a Merit System Contract that clearly spells out the expectations and privileges associated with this status as well as consequences for any violations to the contract.

At this highest level, students have demonstrated the ability to use their social skills successfully and are able to operate without a high need for artificial reinforcers. However, Merit students continue to earn points each day (noncontingent 30,000 point allowance) that enable them to make purchases for tangible or activity reinforcers. Although point earnings are less than on Progress level, Merit students do not need to buy "bonds" and they are also eligible to participate in a variety of activities without having to pay for them.

Merit level students initially carry a smaller Daily Merit card that provides feedback relating to responsible and irresponsible behaviors, homework assignments and areas of extra effort. This is faded to a Weekly Merit card whereby the student would obtain feedback from each of his/her teachers regarding behavior during the past week. After successfully completing 10 consecutive days on the weekly card, Merit students go "off card" and no longer receive a point allowance. This is one of the final steps in the fading process, designed to help students depend less upon points and privileges for using positive social skills and prepare for more inclusive settings. Certainly, however, students would still need to have access to reinforcers although this would be structured similar to that found in regular settings. For a more detailed description of the Boys Town education and motivation system model, the reader is referred to an excellent publication entitled, *Specialized classroom management: A Boys Town approach* (Dowd et al., 1993). There are a number of positive outcome studies that lend support to the Boys Town Model (Bishop, Rosen, Miller & Hendrickson, 1996; Dickson, Thompson, & Swan, 1999; Duppong Hurley & Hylan, 2000; Thompson, Nelson, Spenceri, & Maybank, 1999).

Broad Street Teaching & Learning Center (BSTLC) Level System. Another example of a level system is one that we have developed over the past four years at BSTLC, a special therapeutic day school for children and youth with severe behavioral and emotional disabilities. Simply stated, the BSTLC level system (Coats, 2001) is a program-wide behavior management tool used by students, parents and staff for measuring student success and motivating students to acquire new social and academic skills. Points are awarded or "earned" for meeting basic routine and program rules, demonstrating appropriate social skills and practicing other target behaviors specific to each student. Students earn points and privileges using a four tier level system. Figure 5 shows the levels, point ranges and privileges that are available within each level:

Figure 5 – BSTLC Level System

Levels	Privileges*
Echo (0 – 16 points)	Eyes on supervision & escort No field trip privileges Ineligible for open gym Class store – weekly access
Delta (17 – 24 points)	Partial access (i.e., able to move between classes, group, individual therapy with student pass) No field trip privileges Ineligible for open gym Selected activities at recess or free time Class store – weekly access
Bravo (25 – 27 points)	All Delta privileges Eligible for educational field trips Open gym privileges Video game privileges Extra computer time
Alpha (28 – 30 points)	All Bravo privileges Full access for movement across program settings with student pass Eligible for all field trips (educational & recreational) School store – daily access DVD player access Other selected privileges as determined by teacher

*Note. Privileges may vary as determined by each class.

Procedure. Throughout the school day, students are able to earn points at 30 minute intervals based on a 0 – 3 point performance rating that is awarded immediately following class and transition time. Ratings occur at 10 separate intervals and students can earn up to a maximum total daily score of 30 points. At the end of each class or 30- minute time interval, students are directed to return to their seats and asked to "get ready to rate." Students are then given specific feedback regarding their behavior or performance along with a point rating. In certain cases (i.e., with older or more highly skilled students), points are determined jointly between student and staff. To help increase objectivity with ratings, the following points and criteria are used:

Points	Criteria
3	Excellent; full participation; follows all routines and rules; makes a consistent effort to succeed at individual "target" behaviors
2	Satisfactory; fairly consistent effort; needs only a few reminders or prompts to correct behavior; can be redirected without difficulty
1	Fair; some participation; needs several reminders or limits from staff for inappropriate behavior (e.g., arguing, interrupting others, difficulty with direction following)
0	Poor; no participation; engaged in threatening or disruptive behavior; leaving area of supervision, unexcused absence

Generally speaking, the process of awarding points requires approximately only two to three minutes per class (with six students/class). All points are recorded on a master account sheet maintained in each classroom. Daily totals are later recorded on the students' daily point sheet during the individual teacher-student conference at day's end. The student point sheet (Daily Behavior Report), as shown in Figure 6, provides a summary of the student's performance and interactions throughout the school day and indicates what level the student is on or will advance (decline) to. Students are expected to take their point sheets home to be reviewed and signed by their parent or guardian and then returned the next day.

Figure 6 – Daily Behavior Report

Daily Behavior Report

Student:_____
Date:_____

BEHAVIOR

___Excellent   ___Very Good   ___Good
___Fair   ___Poor   ___Unacceptable

Comments:

SIGNIFICANT EVENTS

	Stayed in class all day		Swearing
	Followed directions		Hands on others
	Accepted help		Screaming / shouting
	Verbal threats / teasing		Hitting others / pushing
	Arguing		Other destructive actions
	Physical threats		Problem focusing / hyper
	Support room		Left area of supervision
	Safe room		Required physical
			restraint

ACADEMICS

	Excellent participation
	Completed all or most work
	Contributed to class discussion
	Completed some work
	Assisted another student
	Completed little or no work

Comments:

Figure 6 continues on the next page

INTERACTIONS   (E) Excellent   (G) Good   (F) Fair
                         (P) Poor

	General attitude_
	Transitions_
	Respect of staff_
	Cooperation_
	Respect of peers
	Respect of self_

TOTAL POINTS EARNED: _____
LEVEL: _____

Staff Signature: _____

Parent/Guardian Signature: _____

Parent/Guardian Comments:

Points may be saved or spent on items available in the class store. Items to be included in the store are typically suggested by students during class meetings and might include such objects as school and art supplies, movie passes, coupons for free ice-cream, music CDs, models and assorted crafts, puzzles, games, small toys, books and magazines. All students, regardless of their level status, may purchase store items when the store is open – generally once each week.

Changing levels. New students to the classroom always begin on Delta level. To advance a level, students must earn and maintain those points required at the next upper level for two consecutive days. For example, a student who is on Echo level must earn at least 17 or higher points for two consecutive days in order to advance to Delta. A student on Delta must earn 25 points or higher to advance to Bravo and so forth. Students may drop a level if they have failed to earn the necessary points. A student may also receive an automatic level drop for engaging in seriously disruptive or dangerous behavior (e.g., fighting, running away, damaging property). Regardless of the points earned, students cannot "skip" any level whether they are advancing or dropping a level. This not only helps students learn the value of persistence and hard work when progressing upward, but also prevents staff from becoming overly negative or punishing as students fail to meet behavioral expectations and drop their level status.

Key Points. When using this type of system, it is important to take the time to review each student's points at the prescribed 30-minute interval. Students with significant social and behavioral disorders tend not to be very competent self-observers and hence, need frequent opportunities to learn about themselves via our specific feedback. At the very least, this helps insure that students receive a relatively high number of interactions per day that focuses on their specific behavioral needs. It is also important to keep the points within the 0 to 3 point range to avoid against "inflation" in the overall system. Bonus points, however, that can be added to a student's savings account can always be awarded for exceptional performance, correcting behaviors or practicing new skills. Finally, the focus should always be positive in the sense that points are *never* to be taken away – only earned. Rather than telling a student that he or she has lost points or that you, as a staff member, are taking them away, your comment should be reframed in a manner that puts the responsibility clearly back on the student (e.g., "Is that behavior helping you earn your points?").

As students demonstrate consistent effort and operate at the upper tiers of the level system over time, they are gradually weaned from reliance on external points to more natural social and activity reinforcers that do not require an exchange of points. For example, students who have achieved at least 30 Alpha days during a marking period (10 weeks) for two consecutive periods or quarters, can be recommended to advance beyond the level system and become an Honor student. Honor students would automatically receive all Alpha level privileges and would be eligible to participate in other special status activities (e.g., providing guest tours, tutoring younger students, engaging in various school leadership events, special celebrations, etc.).

Data collected from both a pilot study and a one-year implementation study of the BSTLC level system involving 20 emotionally disturbed students was highly positive (Coats, 2002).

Results indicated that the frequency of severe behavioral disruptions requiring physical restraint, time out or referral to an alternative support room decreased significantly from pre- to post-treatment conditions following six months of intervention. In addition, teachers reported high satisfaction ratings and indicated that they were able to implement the procedures as designed with minimal difficulty. They also reported that individual student classroom performance improved as a result of the level system although no specific measures of academic achievement were included in the study.

Other Class-wide Systems to Improve Student Behavior

There are numerous practical classroom management strategies for dealing effectively with problem behavior and they often encompass a broad spectrum of behavioral techniques including group contingencies, public posting, token reinforcement, response-cost, and home-school communication. These group support systems often rely on key principles for shaping positive behavioral change: drawing attention to rule-following behavior, utilizing peer influence to encourage positive behavior, and presenting naturally occurring classroom activities and privileges contingently. Some interventions rely on game-like formats that challenge "teams" within a class to compete for rewards contingent upon compliance to rules and displays of other positive behavior. Team-based versus individually based contingencies may be especially helpful for behavior problem students who are likely to receive lower rates of reinforcement from teachers or peers under more traditional classroom reward systems (Forehand & Weirson, 1993). Utilizing peers to encourage appropriate behavior can also increase intervention effectiveness since behavior problem students may be more responsive to peer pressure than to adults who offer inducements to improve their behavior (Rathvon, 1999). Although by no means exhaustive, the following sections describe various class-wide systems that have been found helpful as interventions to increase on-task behavior and reduce inappropriate behavior in the classroom.

The Good Behavior Game. The *Good Behavior Game* (Barrish, Saunders & Wolf, 1969) is a classic example of a highly effective response-cost strategy that uses team competitiveness to reduce disruptive classroom behavior. The basic format involves dividing students into teams that compete for rewards or privileges and assigning them a set number of points at the beginning of the game. The team that receives the fewest number of demerits for specific rule infractions (or has the most points remaining at the end of the game) wins. If both teams receive fewer than a predetermined number of demerits, both teams receive the reward. The intervention has been shown effective with both elementary and special adolescent populations (Barrish et al., 1969; Harris & Sherman, 1973).

After selecting the setting in which the game will be played, it would be important to obtain an initial baseline rate of disruptive behavior in order to establish a basis for determining the number of beginning points to award and the criterion. The procedure could then be implemented as follows:

1. Introduce the intervention by informing students that they will be playing a game designed to help everyone become more successful in class.

2. Demonstrate the procedures and describe the criterion (i.e., the maximum number of demerits allowed) to earn the reward(s). Rewards and privileges typically involve such items as extra free time, extra computer time, no homework pass, movie, etc.

3. Divide the class into two teams. Ideally, teams would have a fairly equal number of disruptive students. Teams could simply be numbered or encouraged to come up with a name to help foster team spirit.

4. Either on a chalkboard or chart, post the team names along with the beginning number of points for each team (e.g., 20), the point criterion (e.g., no fewer than 5 points) and review the class rules. A demerit point would be recorded next to each team when any member on that team violates a rule.

5. At the end of the instructional period, demerit points would be tallied and the team with the least number of demerits would be declared the winner. If both teams exceeded the criterion, both would be winners.

Once students become familiar with the game and behavior improvement is noted, it would be appropriate to gradually lower the limit for demerits or extend the time during which the game is being played. Daily rewards are recommended when first using this type of strategy. Over time and with success, rewards could gradually be faded, for example, to every other day or once per week. There is always the chance that a student or students will declare that they do not want to play the game or will deliberately violate the rules. In this case it might be helpful to create a third team consisting of the problem student or students and then add a negative contingency (e.g., losing teams are deducted 5 minutes of free time for each mark over the criterion).

A variation of *The Good Behavior Game* entitled, *The Good Behavior Game Plus Merit* (Darveaux, 1984) has also been found effective in reducing disruptive behavior as well as in improving academic and social behavior. This strategy combines the use of group contingencies for reducing disruptive behavior with a bonus for improving class participation and academic productivity. Essentially, the same procedures used in *The Good Behavior Game* apply to this game. In addition, however, merit cards or points are given to students who display specific positive target behaviors that have been pre-designated. At the end of the period or game, students are asked to hold up their merit cards to be counted or, as an alternative, the merit points are counted on the board. For every five merits earned, one demerit point is erased for that team. Cards are then collected for future use (or merit points are tallied) and the winners are determined. For example, teams earning less than five demerits receive rewards at the end of the period or day. Again, both teams can win or lose.

Red Light/Green Light. Red Light/Green Light (Rathvon, 1999) is a popular strategy that has been used successfully with young children to reduce off-task and disruptive behavior. It combines continuous visual cues to encourage positive behavior in the context of a group-oriented contingency system.

The basic format requires that students be divided into teams with a fairly even distribution of the most disruptive students across teams. If the students are seated at tables, each table may serve as a team. The intervention requires a flannel board or poster board chart that resembles a "stoplight" and red, yellow and green flannel or paper circles that can be attached to the "stoplight" chart. Each team has a stoplight. A list of classroom rules is also included on or near the chart. The teacher or behavior manager explains that he or she will be observing the teams periodically and using the stoplight charts to rate student behavior according to the following guidelines:

- Teams following rules receive a green light (GO) that indicates they should continue their good behavior.
- Teams that break a rule receive a yellow light (WARNING) that indicates they are being warned to stop the inappropriate behavior.
- Teams that continue to violate the rules or engage in aggressive behavior receive a red light (STOP).
- Teams that are on green at the end of the rating period earn a reward either at the end of the activity, period or day.
- Teams are given a brief description or rationale for their rating.

Response Cost Lottery. The *response cost lottery* is a group method designed to decrease disruptive behavior by offering students opportunities to receive rewards contingent upon displays of appropriate behavior. It was originally tested and found effective with small groups of elementary and middle school students in regular and special education classrooms (Proctor & Morgan, 1991; Witt & Elliott, 1982).

To implement the intervention, students are given a preset number of "lottery" or "raffle" tickets at the start of the class or specific time period. This can be set up as either an independent group contingency where each student receives his/her own tickets with their name written on each or as an interdependent group contingency where students work in teams and each team receives color-coded tickets. Whenever there is a rule violation, the student is told what behavior was inappropriate and one ticket is taken away. In instances where the student argues about the ticket removal or engages in other negative behavior, a second ticket is removed. Continued negative responses would lead to a third ticket being removed and so forth. Toward the end of the period or day, tickets would be collected and, at an established time, a drawing would occur and the student or group of students would select from a menu of prizes. As a variation, the teacher could write "group" on two or more tickets prior to the drawing. If a "group" ticket were selected, the entire class would receive a group prize (e.g., movie, extra free time, pizza, etc.). Lottery drawings could be held daily or weekly.

Public Posting to Increase Positive Student Behavior.
This is a fairly generic strategy that utilizes a positive and
independent group contingency to decrease disruptive behavior
and increase appropriate student behavior. It is particularly suited
for smaller self-contained class settings and can be implemented
across the school day. Very simply, the intervention involves
public posting of the classroom rules along with student names
(i.e., on a grid format). During the specified class period or
interval, students who are following rules receive a check, star or
sticker by their name. Only one check would be earned per
interval. Particularly with younger children, publicly posting stars
or stickers can add visual reinforcement for positive behavior. An
initial criterion necessary for earning a reward from a menu would
be established and students would then receive the reward based
on their interval or daily performance. As with most
reinforcement systems, the specific methods used (e.g., points,
stickers, amount and type of rewards, etc.) are limited only by the
creativity of the teacher or behavior manager.

A Potpourri of Strategies.   There are obviously many
approaches to group management that can be used either as an
isolated strategy (e.g., time out) or in combination with multiple
strategies (e.g., time out and token reinforcement). Public posting
of rules and charting, token systems, variations of time out,
response cost and home-note programs are just some of the
approaches found to be effective in reducing disruptive behavior,
improving social behavior and increasing academic productivity.
Again, however, it is beyond the scope of this book to review
these in any detail. For more information on this subject, the
reader is referred to a number of other readings (Blechman, 1985;
Cohen & Fish, 1993; Rathvon, 1999; Rhode & Jenson, 1993;
Sprick & Howard, 1995; Sprick, Sprick & Garrison, 1993;
Stewart, 2002; Wielkiewicz, 1986).

SUMMARY
        This chapter highlights key features or elements of
effective group management plans. Plan developers need to have
a shared understanding of those behaviors they wish to promote.
They must also have clearly defined behavioral expectations along
with a set of well-defined consequences for engaging in positive
and negative behavior.   In addition, there should be a

programmatic effort to help students learn skills necessary for self-control, problem-solving and positive social behavior. Without this perspective, a program will be unlikely to create any meaningful or lasting behavior change. Regardless of the group management plan that exists, staff must maintain a commitment to developing strong student-teacher relationships within the context of a learning environment that engages students in meaningful instructional activities.

As with individual management plans, group plans are often most effective when the design and selection of strategies occurs as a collaborative process and when there exists a clear understanding of goals. Steps necessary in developing group management plans are described along with suggestions for consideration during the design phase.

Finally, various structured reinforcement systems are described including level systems, token economies and game-based systems.

CHAPTER 7

RESPONDING TO BEHAVIORAL CRISES

In special programs that serve children and adolescents with emotional disturbance, having a plan for crisis management should not be viewed as an afterthought but as a necessity and an integral component of the program. Indeed, all schools today are at risk for crises and need to be prepared to organize and respond effectively in the face of a crisis. Largely, as a result of the growing number of multiple school shootings in U.S. schools, many school districts across the country have developed their own crisis intervention plans. Typically, these plans often address such features as school evacuation procedures, security methods, administrative chains of command and dealing with the aftermath of a crisis. While these organizational issues are certainly important, the focus of this chapter will look more closely at methods of intervening with students whose behavior may deteriorate to a more violent or disruptive level.

Perhaps one of the most pronounced features of a crisis in the schools is the intense emotionality and "disequilibrium" experienced by the system (Poland & Pitcher, 1990). In systems that are not prepared, staff members can experience any number of feelings including helplessness, fear, inadequacy and confusion. Potential long-term negative effects can result in staff burnout, physical symptoms and a breakdown in functional working relationships. Therefore, it is critical that school programs establish crisis intervention procedures that address effective coping and management behavior during periods of extreme emotionality. Any response to a crisis situation must not only be well planned but also capable of being implemented safely and professionally. Crises will happen - the enraged child who throws a chair, the frustrated teen who verbally abuses staff, or the agitated youngster who punches or bangs his head in self-abusive fashion. Each of these situations requires some form of immediate attention and response from staff.

CRISIS DEVELOPMENT

Traditionally, crises have been viewed as unfolding in four stages: Initially, there is an increase in tension due to the crisis event. Next, in the face of continued stress, tension escalates because the usual problem-solving strategies are unsuccessful. Third, additional problem-solving resources are mobilized and as a result of the failure of these, the final phase of emotional breakdown occurs (Caplan, 1964). With respect to disruptive student behavior, I view crisis situations as generally narrow segments in time when an individual is in need of increased supervision or protection. The individual may be threatening harm to himself or others. He or she may be highly anxious, verbally abusive or, in extreme cases, physically assaultive. Chances are that the individual at this point has lost rational and physical control. These highly charged situations can look very chaotic and to the untrained person, they probably are. However, crises also have recognizable stages that can serve to guide staff in determining what might be the most appropriate response. As I had described earlier in Chapter Three, our crisis management system at BSTLC is based on the *Non-Violent Crisis Intervention (CPI)* Model (Wyka & Gabriel, 1983). Within this model staff are trained to be able to recognize different levels or stages of crisis development. The response to each stage is very different.

Perhaps one of the most valuable features of the CPI model is the practical framework it provides for understanding crisis development that differs somewhat from the outline described by Caplan (1964). Although on a surface level one might view a crisis situation as being unpredictable and chaotic, it often is not. For the purpose of instruction, the CPI model depicts the initial stage of crisis as a period of increased agitation or anxiety that escalates in intensity to a point when a person releases significant amounts of verbal and/or physical energy. In other words, a crisis is likely to begin long before that moment in time when the person acts out.

As a core feature of the CPI model, Caraulia and Steiger (1997) describe four distinct stages in crisis development that represent an individual's internal conflict that he or she may escalate through. The model also includes descriptions of the appropriate corresponding staff response at each level that is designed to avoid an over- or under-reaction on the part of staff. Figure 7 provides an outline of their crisis development model.

Figure 7 - Stages in Crisis Development

Crisis Level:	*Staff Behavior:*
1. Anxiety	1. Supportive
2. Verbal aggression	2. Setting Limits/Directive
3. Physical aggression	3. Personal safety/Physical restraint
4. Tension reduction	4. Postvention/Debriefing

Anxiety Stage

The initial stage – Anxiety – refers to some degree of noticeable change in a person's behavior or energy level. This change is likely to be non-directed and observable through nonverbal communication (e.g., fidgeting, pacing, playing with an object, etc.). Staff who are able to recognize the early warning signs of anxious behavior and respond in a supportive manner may be able to defuse a potentially dangerous situation. Being supportive often involves taking an empathic, nonjudgmental perspective and, perhaps most importantly, being a good listener. Empathic listening is probably one of the most powerful tools you can use when intervening with an anxious person. To be an empathic listener requires a very active response. If you can listen and not advise, give your undivided attention, reflect the person's feelings, and use silence and restatement, you may very well assist the individual in terms of reducing defensiveness and improving his or her thinking. Often at this point, it is also critical to pay attention to such matters as your own personal space, body language and gestures and voice tone. These are all features an agitated individual is likely to be keying in on and it's important that you do not come across as a threat.

Verbal Aggression/Defensive Stage

Unfortunately, there are times when a supportive response is not enough and the individual escalates to the second level – Verbal Aggression and Defensive. It is not uncommon for the individual at this level to begin to lose the ability to think rationally and engage in more challenging, limit-testing behavior. For example, noncompliance to staff directives, challenges to a person's authority, verbal threats of violence and intense verbal outbursts are behaviors often seen at this level. In response to this type of defensive behavior, Caraulia and Steiger (1997) emphasize the importance of taking a directive stance that involves setting limits.

Setting limits refers to a brief description of the rules and standards of appropriate as well as inappropriate behavior that your school or program defines. It also defines the consequences for abiding by or violating these standards. For an individual who may be losing rational control, it helps establish the boundaries within which that person can learn to behave in an acceptable manner. Simply stated, limit-setting is a process in which an individual is given choices and their corresponding consequences in response to a directive you have issued.

There is no doubt that limit-setting can be a difficult task. Many adults who work in the human services field struggle with this particular skill often because they have not received training in this process. However, with practice and an adherence to a few key principles, most people can become effective limit-setters. To do so requires the use of certain underlying principles when setting limits. As much as possible, limits and consequences should be clear, concise, reasonable and, most importantly, enforceable. If you are not specific in your directive, there is an increased risk that the individual will not comply or fully understand what behavior is inappropriate. Don't assume the person knows this. If your limit is too complex or difficult to understand, you run the risk that the person will become confused and even escalate. Keep your directives simple (e.g., two choices rather than five). If your limit is unreasonable or not in line with your program policies, you will most likely be unable to enforce the consequences and, again, increase the chances of escalation. Obviously, if you cannot enforce your limit, it will be meaningless and you will lose credibility as a professional who can adequately meet the student's needs.

There are many things to avoid when setting limits. Arguing, demanding immediate compliance, interrupting, belittling, and issuing threatening statements are all staff behaviors to avoid. However, by maintaining an attitude that communicates respect along with a sense of care for the individual in crisis, staff will be more likely to de-escalate the situation and preserve the student-staff relationship.

Although there is no one correct way to issue limits, there are certain guidelines that may prove helpful. I often think of these guidelines as a "personal formula" or strategy that can be followed and practiced. The following steps provide an outline of this strategy:

1) Describe the inappropriate behavior.
2) Give a rationale as to why the behavior is inappropriate.
3) Offer reasonable choices and consequences; state the positive first.
4) Allow time (if possible) to avoid an ultimatum.
5) Enforce consequences.

Let's take the example of a student who, in a group session, is inappropriately touching another student sitting next to him. If we were to use the above formula, the limit could be delivered in the following way:

1) "Dan, you're sitting too close to Robert and poking him." *(behavioral description)*
2) "That's distracting to everyone including you." *(rationale)*
3) "If you can give yourself more space and stop touching him, you'll be able to stay in group and earn points." If you keep poking Robert, you'll have to sit out of our group and will not earn all of your points." *(choices and consequences)*
4) "Make a good choice." *(allowing time)*
5) "Dan, thanks for listening to the direction. I'm glad you decided to stay in group today." *(enforcing consequences)*

It is important to remember that you will not always gain compliance even when you do your best at setting limits. After all, no one can make anyone do anything and you are not responsible for another person's behavior. Remember also that you have not failed if the person does not comply with your directive. What is most helpful to understand is that by consistently enforcing your consequences, you will increase the chances that the individual will comply in the future. Limits that are delivered on a consistent basis help establish a structure by which the person can learn that behaviors and choices are accompanied by consequences (National Crisis Prevention

Institute,1991).

Physical Aggression Stage

At times, despite our best efforts at defusing another person's behavior, that person may lose control and escalate to the third stage in crisis development, the Physical Acting Out level. This person may attempt to assault others, damage property or possibly harm himself. What may be the most appropriate intervention at this point could be the use of physical restraint that involves taking control of another person's body and keeping that person safe.

Certainly, physically restraining a person is dangerous and must always be taken seriously. In certain situations, the most prudent action may be for staff to remove themselves as well as other students and call for emergency assistance (e.g., law enforcement). Law enforcement officials generally have more training to handle violent situations, often work in teams and carry weapons (if necessary). If a person enters the front doors of school wielding a handgun, a hands-off response would be wise. However, the same response would probably not be appropriate if a student was fighting with another student. With the appropriate training and staff, physical intervention can be the most effective response taken for the sole purpose of keeping everyone safe.

At the very least, the management of out of control behavior is a crucial task in the treatment of seriously disturbed children and youth. The reassurance for the child that he or she will be protected from hurting himself or others is a basic premise of all therapy. Therefore, physical restraint must never be used as a punitive measure nor should it be pain inflicting. The appropriate use of any behavioral control such as restraint or isolation time out should occur only in the context of having a thorough understanding of the child's unique emotional status and needs (Bridge et al., 1986).

While situations that require physical restraint can be dangerous and highly stressful, there are certain actions that staff can take to reduce the overall level of stress. The following tips may offer help in such situations:

- Remember that restraint is not a form of aggression because it is controlled. By reminding yourself that, as a trained staff member, you are utilizing a therapeutic technique to keep the student, yourself and others safe, you are better able to remain calm and emotionally detached.

- Try to monitor your own voice tone and expression with the student as well as with other staff. It is often best to say as little as possible until the situation is more controlled. While you may be feeling highly anxious yourself, try to project a sense of calmness. An agitated person is much more likely to pay attention to your nonverbal behavior (body language and voice tone) than to your words.

- Understand what words or actions are likely to escalate you. In other words, know your own "buttons" so you can disarm them. Remember, in a majority of instances, you are simply a safe and convenient target. Knowing this can help maintain an attitude of detachment that will most likely increase your effectiveness in the situation.

- Try to work in teams. Having another staff member is always recommended in order to reduce the risk of personal injury to staff or student, assist with other crisis-related tasks (e.g., removing peers) or serve as a witness.

- Know your environment and use it to your advantage. Be alert to potential weapons that could be used by the student (e.g., scissors, ruler, pens, pencils, etc.) and remove them if possible.

- Monitor your own physical contact with the student to insure that you are providing a message that is consistent with your words and tone. Also, don't hold a student too long. Students need to see that calming down results in being released.

- Students should be released gradually and gently rather than abruptly. In advance, it may be helpful to inform the student that he or she will be released. This is also a time when the student can be given directions that allows him/her to know what will happen next.

Any program that serves emotionally disturbed children and youth has a serious responsibility to provide training and supervision for all staff who may be called upon to do physical restraints. For more detailed information and assistance on this subject, the reader is encouraged to learn more about the CPI model (Wyka & Gabriel, 1983) or others (CALM Training, 1997; Professional Assault Response Training, 2002; Satori Alternatives to Managing Aggression, 1999; SCIP-R Training: NYS Office of Mental Retardation & Developmental Disabilities, undated; Therapeutic Crisis Intervention program: Residential Child Care Project – Family Life Development Center, 2002) that offer training and provide therapeutic guidelines for the appropriate use of restraint techniques.

Tension Reduction Stage

The last stage in crisis development, Tension Reduction, is that point in time when the individual begins to calm down and regain rational thought (Caraulia & Steiger, 1997). This individual would no longer be acting out physically because high levels of energy cannot be sustained indefinitely. Generally, the person's defenses are down which increases the chances for improved compliance to staff directives. You may also see other emotional signs including crying, expressions of remorse, embarrassment, anxiety and anger.

It is extremely important to work with the person at this level because of the unique opportunity that exists for promoting growth and behavioral change. It also helps staff re-establish communication and rapport with the person who acted out. These attempts to establish "therapeutic rapport" (Wyka & Gabriel, 1983) have been referred to as postvention. While this is not a substitute for individual counseling, postvention can set the stage for other interventions including counseling or therapy. A more detailed look at this process is outlined in the sections that follow.

RESPONDING TO CRISIS

Plans

Before a crisis erupts, there should be a plan in place. Ideally, the plan should be flexible yet capable of answering the following questions: What behavior(s) or incident would require a team intervention? Who is to be contacted to be a part of the team and how? Who would be the team leader? Where might students be taken who are not directly involved in the crisis situation? Who would be responsible for postvention work and documenting the incident?

As another proactive measure, planning activities should also include at least some degree of self-reflection among staff members. For example, maintaining your own personal emotional control during a crisis is a critical factor that can increase the chances for a more positive outcome. Emotional control, often referred to as "rational detachment," is a necessary condition that allows staff to remain in control and address the needs of students. Caraulia & Steiger describe this as "the ability to depersonalize a crisis situation by staying calm and in control" (Caraulia & Steiger, 1997, p.130). It is important to recognize the "emotional buttons" that set you off and cause you to become less than professional in your actions. Unfortunately, when staff get hooked and lose control, they compromise their ability to intervene safely and effectively. Although the causes of acting out behavior may be beyond our control and students may escalate to a physical level despite our best efforts, we can still learn to control our responses to these events.

Thinking through a plan in advance and developing new skills will not only improve staff confidence and professionalism but also minimize the risk of panic during an actual crisis event. It would be naïve to think that all crisis situations can be predicted and that your best efforts at planning will work 100% of the time. However, failing to take the time to develop a crisis plan and examine your own attitudes, will more than likely work against you and lead to greater chaos.

Alternative Settings within the Program
Isolation Time Out / Safe Room. The need for a safe, quiet, low stimulus area or room is often considered essential in programs serving emotionally and behaviorally disordered students. Indeed, in many crisis situations, the use of isolation time out is often a necessary intervention for students who are a serious threat to themselves or others. As mentioned earlier in Chapter 5, any use of an isolation time out room should be offered as an option in a non-punitive manner. It should only be utilized in order to help students remain safe, minimize potential feelings of shame, guilt or trauma as a result of their aggression and to protect out-of-control students from negative peer reactions. The primary purpose should be to assist the student to become calm and reorganize (mentally) at a higher level of functioning in order to cope more adaptively (Bridge et al., 1986).

As a minimum, programs that use isolation or

seclusionary time out need to establish objective guidelines and procedures to assure appropriate use. Based on recent research and practice in the field, guidance from the Office of special Education Programs, United States Department of Education and court cases on the subject, the following guidelines are offered:

1. Isolation time out should only be used for behaviors that are dangerous to self and/or others, destructive of property or are severely disruptive to the milieu. It would not be an appropriate intervention in response to simple noncompliance, use of obscenities, academic refusal, etc.

2. Parent / guardian permission to use time out should be obtained before using this as an intervention. A discussion should clearly specify the procedures that will be used, including factors that would warrant use of time out.

3. Isolation time out should only occur after less restrictive methods have been used and documented as ineffective in reducing negative behavior. As discussed in Chapter 5, time out should be considered as only one component of an extensive array of behavior interventions. It should never be used in isolation as the only intervention applied.

4. The use of isolation time out should be reviewed, approved and included as part of the student's individual education or 504 plan.

5. Excessive use of time out should be avoided. Depending on the age of the child, students should not be secluded in a time out setting for more than 5 to 10 minutes and never more than 15 minutes in total. Continued use of seclusionary time out must be based on data supporting its effectiveness in reducing problem behavior. If such data is not present, this procedure should not be used.

6. Isolation time out rooms must never be locked. Staff must be able to continuously observe and have access to the student.

7. Each use of isolation time out must be documented and regularly reviewed as part of the student's overall treatment plan. In addition to the student's name, the behavior log should include the date, time in and time out, a brief description of antecedent events or reason for referral, whether restraint was involved, and staff initials.

Such documentation can be used in evaluating the success of the intervention, determining patterns of behavior or recognizing when adaptations may be necessary. When time out is not effective, an FBA would be indicated.

8. The school, program or agency is responsible for providing adequate training and supervision for staff who implement this level of intervention.

Support Rooms. As a component to any crisis plan, the utilization of a temporary alternative setting – apart from isolation time out - for an agitated, disruptive or anxious student can be part of an effective intervention plan. For example, Glasser (1990) referred to this type of setting as a *planning room* where students would go in order to "make a plan to do better" before they could return to class. At BSTLC, we refer to this setting as a *support room* because of its' intended function as a supportive and therapeutic environment for agitated or emotionally fragile students. Unlike isolation time out, students who are referred to "support" are generally capable of following verbal directions and are, for the most part, safe.

In terms of implementation, we utilize the services of a certified school social worker and an assistant who work directly with referred students. The room itself is similar in size to other classrooms and is especially designed to give students their own space (i.e., a floor to ceiling study carrel) as well as a common area with chairs and table used for conferencing and mediation work. While at their carrels, students are not in visible contact with other students yet are capable of being visibly monitored by staff. Approximately three to five students can be accommodated at any given time.

Support rooms can be used for a variety of purposes, including:

- Preventing the student from interacting with peers. Often, peer attention and approval can serve as a powerful reinforcer for inappropriate behavior.
- Affording the student an opportunity to reflect upon the problem in a calm, reserved atmosphere that can lead to increased acceptance of personal responsibility.
- Providing students with an appropriate alternative to acting out as part of their own safety plan (i.e., in cases of

self or teacher-directed referrals).

- Counseling the student about alternative strategies. This enables the student to learn coping strategies to deal with situations that may occur in the future.

- Enabling the student to complete academic assignments because of increased adult support and fewer distractions.

- Enabling staff, through periodic analyses of behavior logs, to identify patterns of behavior that may result in changes to the student's behavior management plan or recommendations for class/program changes or additional support services.

The guidelines for support room use should, of course, be made very clear. Theoretically, such a location should not be used as a form of punishment where students are chastised for their behavior or subjected to arbitrary penalties. Instead, it should be used as a meaningful consequence where students can calm down, feel safe, accept responsibility for their behavior and engage in problem-solving. Staff should accompany all students who are referred and, as clearly and concisely as possible, state the reason for referral. Particularly in the presence of an agitated student, there should be limited dialogue with the student until there has been sufficient time to cool down (for both staff and student). If appropriate, it may be helpful to engage the student in some type of self-calming activity (e.g., drawing, coloring, using clay, puzzles, magazines, deep breathing, etc), talking with an adult, or just sitting quietly. In cases where the student may require extended time (e.g., one or two hours), it may be helpful to have student academic work available.

Once the student begins to calm down and displays improved rational control, the support room or other appropriate staff can then discuss with the student what led to the referral and establish the criteria for returning to class. It should be expected that all interactions be calm, courteous and respectful. Ideally, the atmosphere can be characterized as being serious, yet friendly. Clear communication among those staff members involved is essential in order to establish reasons for the student's referral and what is expected for the student's return to class. At BSTLC, we have found it helpful to include the referring staff, support room staff, and student, when appropriate, in determining when to re-enter the classroom.

Teams

In programs that either have sufficient staffing or a designated staff who are available to intervene in crisis situations, formal teams are already established. However, in many programs including ours at BSTLC, team member selection is not predetermined because, owing to the unpredictable nature of crisis situations, not everyone is likely to be on the premises when a crisis erupts. We have found it extremely helpful to train a majority of the staff including non-professional support staff (e.g., custodians, secretaries) in the CPI model and techniques. Obviously, this allows for greater flexibility when responding to unpredictable crisis situations since the "team" is not dependent upon the presence of any one particular person. Teams generally involve fewer than five members. Having too many team members present can be confusing and can create greater anxiety on the part of the acting out student. This, in turn, can increase the chances that the situation will become worse.

Summoning a crisis response team should obviously be done as easily and efficiently as possible. There are several different ways of doing this. Some facilities use silent alarms or a public address system with a subtle code. Others use two-way radios, a telephone or intercom system to request assistance. Probably the simplest method is to send a bystander (i.e., staff member or student) to seek help.

Team Leader Duties. All crisis teams need to have a leader who can direct the action of others involved on the team. Again, because of the fluid nature of team composition, a leader usually changes from one situation to another and is often selected on the scene in response to the question – "Who is the team leader?" As Caraulia and Steiger (1997) suggest, a team leader may be selected based on several different criteria. This person may be the first to arrive on the scene and therefore in a better position to assess the situation and develop a plan of action. Another factor may relate to the level of confidence and skill held by a team member. It can also be advantageous if the team member selected knows the acting out individual and has already established some level of rapport with this person. In some instances, we have found it helpful for the team leadership to change by "handing off" this responsibility to another team member who may be more effective in the situation. Via either direct or coded messages, other team members must be made aware of this change.

The duties of a team leader in the CPI model are comprehensive and include the following:

1) Assess the situation – How dangerous is the situation? Are weapons involved? Is the student anxious or irrational? Do I need more staff assistance? Should the police be involved?

2) Develop a plan – This generally involves deciding what needs to be done to resolve the situation safely and determining specific roles for team members.

3) Direct the team – The team leader must be very clear in directing other members on the team. This is not the time for building consensus.

4) Communication with the acting out individual – The team leader or someone designated by the team leader should talk with the acting out individual. Keeping communication limited to one person eliminates confusion and helps the acting out individual focus on what is being said.

At BSTLC, we also assign the team leader the task of ensuring that important follow-up work is done. If a physical restraint intervention occurred, the student would be assessed and, if necessary, treated by the school nurse. In all instances the team leader would make certain that proper documentation of the incident occurs and that parents and other staff as appropriate are contacted.

Postvention

Postvention with the student is another primary objective in the aftermath of a crisis because it leads to the re-establishment of communication with the person who has acted out. This involves making certain that the student, once calm and rational, is given the opportunity to discuss what happened in order to learn from the experience and gain a sense of closure. This is also a critical time in which to give the student much needed encouragement and support - what Caraulia and Steiger refer to as the establishment of "therapeutic rapport." The CPI *coping* model (Crisis Prevention Institute, 1988) outlines the steps that can lead to the development of therapeutic rapport via student debriefing.

Each letter of the *coping* model represents various conditions and actions that must occur. Key features of the model include the following:

> Control – Before a crisis can be discussed, everyone needs to be rational and in control both physically and emotionally.
>
> Orient – The student needs to be oriented to the facts. Clarify what happened.
>
> Patterns – It is important to determine the presence or absence of any patterns to the person's behavior.
>
> Investigate – This is where staff can explore possible solutions with the student.
>
> Negotiate – The focus is on negotiating for change and setting small goals.
>
> Give – The final action is to give back a sense of control or ownership to the student in order to signal closure and provide encouragement and support (Wyka & Gabriel, 1983).

After a crisis, it is also important to conduct a team debriefing meeting. This enables team members to discuss the events that occurred including what led up to the crisis, how effective the team intervention was, and ways to improve team operations. Especially after a very difficult incident, it can be extremely helpful to give members an opportunity to discuss the facts and their feelings about what happened and to receive support from those who were involved. It is not uncommon for team members to feel angry at the student or with a co-worker about his or her involvement. Staff may feel embarrassed about their own performance or begin to doubt their ability to intervene effectively in future situations. Consequently, debriefing meetings can be an effective vehicle used to improve team performance and staff rapport. As suggested by Caraulia and Steiger (1997), there are a number of questions that can be asked during a debriefing session:

- What were members thinking and feeling during or after the crisis?
- How was the team contacted and did this occur in a timely fashion?
- Was a team leader identified and did others know who this

person was?
- Did the team leader give clear directives?
- If physical restraint was used, how did team members respond?
- Was only one person (i.e., team leader) speaking to the acting out individual?
- Were team members able to depersonalize the situation?
- Was the best possible "care, welfare, safety and security" given to everyone that was involved in the crisis situation?

Behaviors that Pose a Safety Risk

Programs that serve children and youth with behavioral disorders must be prepared to address a variety of behaviors that pose a safety risk either to the individual student or others. This might involve assault (physical, sexual, psychological) or serious injury toward a student or staff member. Many schools have established advisory or safety committees that are responsible for developing plans that can address potentially dangerous incidents that may extend beyond individual student situations. There is no question that as crises become epidemic, the need for effective crisis response capabilities becomes obvious.

In response to this need, Critical Incident Stress Management (CISM) has become one of the most powerful and cost-effective approaches to crisis intervention (Everly, Flannery & Mitchell, in press). CISM is a comprehensive, integrative, multicomponent program that works to decrease the effects of critical incident stress before problems become rooted. While it was originally developed for use in the emergency services professions, CISM is now becoming a "standard of care" in many schools (Everly & Mitchell, 1997). At BSTLC, we have found this model to be effective in reducing traumatic stress effects. Regardless of the systems involved, programs should have in place clear guidelines to address safety-related problems. The following scenarios represent potential critical incidents that may require implementation of critical incident stress management procedures.

Leaving the Building or Campus Without Permission. In a majority of cases, it may not be best to pursue the student who has left the grounds as this may serve to reinforce negative attention getting behavior and intensify the problem situation. However, an assessment should be made by the crisis team as to the feasibility of returning the student to the building. In the event that the student does not return, the administrator should be notified and appropriate follow-up action taken (e.g., police and parent/guardian contacted). Implementation of consequences as stated in the program or individual behavior management plan would occur.

Vandalism. Many oppositional and aggressive students choose to vent their frustration and hostility on objects rather than the situations or people who have contributed to their feelings. Doors, walls, windows and furniture are often those items that suffer the most. Vandalism should always be documented and reported to the administration. Restitution, in the form of repayment or repair, would be a logical consequence as might other consequences that are included in a school's code of conduct or behavior management plan.

Threats of Violence. All threats of violence and violent actions need to be taken seriously. In many cases, threatening statements and posturing on the part of an agitated student signals that aggressive action is not far behind. Staff would be wise at such a point to summon help or call for crisis team assistance. An assessment of the situation could be made with team member input and appropriate action taken (e.g., parent notification, removal to an alternative setting, suspension, police involvement, hospitalization).

Weapons Possession. Obviously, weapons in any form are strictly forbidden and must be turned into the building administration. What is perhaps most important is to be proactive. Most schools and facilities have clearly defined emergency response systems in place to prevent or respond in an organized manner to situations involving weapons. Possession of firearms or incinerary devices is a very serious offense. If weapons are used, this clearly presents a crisis situation and an appropriate team intervention or critical incident response should occur. The first concern should be the removal of students and staff out of harms way. Again, all facilities should have a very clear plan established that is practiced on a routine basis (e.g., school safety plans, emergency evacuation, lock down procedures).

SUMMARY

Responding to crisis situations is never easy and, in many cases, dangerous. However, by improving our understanding of crisis development, having a plan, maintaining a positive attitude and learning new skills, it is likely that we can be more successful in de-escalating potential crisis situations. Maintaining an attitude of rational detachment is a key objective because it enables staff to respond without under or over-reacting to situations. By establishing a positive attitude and staying in control, team members will be in a better position to meet the safety and security needs of those individuals involved in crisis. All schools and programs need to have well-defined safety plans for dealing with critical incidents in an effort to achieve the goal of crisis stabilization and symptom mitigation.

CHAPTER 8

PROGRAM EVALUATION

WHAT IS PROGRAM EVALUATION?

High-quality programs that serve the needs of children and youth, invest time and resources for measuring outcome effectiveness. In particular, many nonprofit organizations and schools are increasingly interested in outcome measurement (McNamara, 1998) and a growing number of governmental agencies, funding sources, and the public are calling for better accountability for the use of resources (Hatry, van Houten, Plantz & Taylor, 1996). Although the push for accountability has been a primary factor in outcome measurement, a more fundamental purpose for measuring outcomes is to see if the program really makes a difference in the lives of people.

Evaluation data provide information or findings that can help programs adapt, improve and become more effective. The potential benefits of program evaluation are almost unlimited. Data can be used to strengthen existing programs and services, target services for expansion, eliminate or modify ineffective programs, streamline service delivery, increase staff morale and support, recruit talented staff, gain favorable public recognition, retain or increase funding, and encourage program development through the dissemination of information to other potential users.

What exactly is program evaluation? In simplest terms, program evaluation is the systematic collection and analysis of data about a program or some aspect of a program in order to make decisions. It is the foundation of any program improvement effort. An evaluation may involve needs assessments, cost/benefit analyses, formative, summative, goal-based, process or outcome-based assessment (McNamara, 1998). There are a wide variety of methods that can be used and there are numerous books and materials that focus on evaluation designs, methods and techniques of analysis (Fetterman, 2001; Fetterman, Kafterian & Wandersman, 1996; Hatry et al., 1996; Puckett & Vogt, 1995).

Fortunately, program evaluation does not have to be an overwhelming process and those interested in or responsible for conducting evaluations need not be experts on these subjects. This chapter provides basic guidance for measuring program outcomes and using the results in a very practical and realistic fashion. Ideally, program personnel can play a key role in deciding what to examine, conducting the evaluation and interpreting the results. Much of the information contained in this chapter comes from the various works of Patton (1987), McNamara (1998), Goodwill Industries (1994) and the United Way of America (1996).

TYPES OF PROGRAM EVALUATION

There are many kinds or dimensions of evaluation that can be useful to programs including process, outcome, and impact evaluation (Muraskin, 1998). Process evaluations examine program materials and activities. They are generally geared toward understanding how a program works and identifying its strengths and weaknesses. For example, staff might systematically review the units in an anger management curriculum to determine whether they adequately address those behaviors the program seeks to influence. Process evaluation might also involve examining the implementation of program activities and how students respond or whether services have been delivered in an appropriate and efficient manner. A primary purpose in this method of evaluation is to improve service delivery where needed.

Outcomes-based evaluations are generally conducted in order to find out whether a program is effective or "makes a difference" for service recipients. In other words, is there an immediate or direct effect seen in the behavior of students as a result of the program? An outcomes evaluation examines the impacts, benefits and changes to program recipients (or students) as a result of the program's efforts during and/or after their participation in the program. For example, you may want to examine changes or outcomes that are expressed in terms of knowledge or skills (often considered short-term outcomes), behaviors (intermediate outcomes) or values or status (long-term outcomes). Similarly, you may want to consider looking at outcome targets such as the number or percentage of students who achieved a certain outcome. Another method may involve the examination of outcome indicators that can tell you whether you're making any progress toward you're outcome goal or target (e.g., the number of students who had no suspensions right after the program and three months after the program).

Impact evaluations are in many ways similar to outcome studies that look beyond the immediate results of instruction and services to identify longer-term and sometimes unintended effects. For example, an impact evaluation might examine whether students who were discharged from a program were able to succeed in less restrictive educational settings over time or whether or not they required psychiatric hospitalization.

Regardless of the specific outcomes or kind of evaluation you may wish to pursue, the data to be collected must be valid and reliable. A measure is valid only to the degree that it actually measures what it claims to measure. A measure is reliable to the degree that its' meaning is stable or consistent over time. In other words, if the same measure (e.g., questionnaire, test) is used again with the same individual or group, it should yield a similar score. Data collected can be quantitative or qualitative depending upon the questions you wish to answer. Successful evaluations often include both forms. What is important to understand is that there is often more than one way to answer any given question.

COMMON MYTHS

Unfortunately, many myths exist in regard to program evaluation. Many believe that evaluation is a useless, academic activity that demands excessive time commitments and generates data with little utility. To the contrary, evaluation should be an ongoing process that involves activities you are already doing. It should be integrated into the structure of a program rather than seen as something added on after the fact. Good evaluations also yield information that helps define how successful your program is in terms of reaching its' objectives and in identifying areas that need further attention.

Many also believe that evaluation is a highly complex process that requires the use of outside experts. As mentioned above, this is not necessarily the case. Those interested in program evaluation do not need to be Ph.D. level data analysts or psychometric experts who are versed in statistical methods of evaluation design and data analyses. However, those interested in evaluation do need to consider what information they should collect in order to make decisions about program needs or issues. Rather than a whole new set of activities that requires additional resources, an outcomes evaluation process can be part of normal management activities that are carried out routinely. Essentially, there must be a commitment to understanding what is going on in your program. Concerns about "doing it the right versus the wrong way" should also be dispelled. Just remember that any effort to measure program effectiveness is better than no effort at all. It is often best to start simple and learn as you go along in terms of your evaluation plan and implementation.

Others believe that evaluation is simply about proving the success or failure of a program. Unfortunately, there is no perfect program and a simple pass / fail score would provide little, if any, useful information. In real life, success has more to do with remaining open to continuous feedback and making adjustments based on this feedback.

Finally, some believe that they already know whether their program is meeting the needs of their clients or students. In the real world, this may or may not be the case. Good data does not lie. Outcomes evaluations will at least help ensure that you will know the needs of your clients because it sets up structures in your organization that keeps you focused on current needs.

PLANNING YOUR PROGRAM EVALUATION

Although the task of conducting a program evaluation may seem overly complex, it need not be. Typically, when planning any program evaluation there are a few basic questions to be answered, such as:

- For what purpose is the evaluation being done? (i.e., What decisions do you want to be able to make as a result of the evaluation?)
- Who are the primary audiences for the results of the evaluation? (staff, board members, clients, students, parents, funders)
- What kinds of information are needed to demonstrate program effectiveness?
- From what sources should the information be collected? (students, parents, staff, archival records, etc.)

- What methods will be used to collect information? (observations, questionnaires, interviews, focus groups, examination of records, tests, etc.)
- What resources exist to collect, analyze and report the data?
- How can the information be reported in useful fashion?

The United Way of America (1996) provides a very helpful guide in reference to outcomes-based evaluation and describes an eight-step approach to developing a system for measuring outcomes and using the results. Readers are encouraged to review this manual for more information on this topic. However, there are many different processes and procedures that can be used in planning program evaluations and the decision as to what model to use will vary depending upon your program or agency needs and resources. The following sections provide an outline of those steps and decisions necessary for evaluation planning. The outline is written in a manner that applies to diverse programs and makes no assumptions about program size, budgetary support, program goals and mission, student characteristics or staff competence in conducting program evaluations.

GETTING STARTED

Most likely, one of the first steps is to decide which program or aspect of a program will be measured. With schools or other human service agencies, an outcome-based evaluation is often the model of choice because it can lead to an improvement in services. Perhaps more importantly and, as stated earlier, it can also indicate whether or not the program actually makes a difference. In addition to determining what program to measure, it is important to identify who exactly will be the evaluation's consumers. This will help in determining what questions to ask, what data will be credible, what analyses should be done and how the results should be presented.

Although one person may be in charge of the evaluation, it may be helpful to assemble a work group or committee to plan and implement the outcome measurement process. Putting together a small work group (e.g., 3 to 5 members) will not only reduce the burden for one individual but also help insure that all issues can be considered from different perspectives. Ideally, this group can communicate and seek input from all staff in reference to many important issues including:

- Why the program is going to measure outcomes.
- What outcomes it will measure.
- Data or indicators that will be used to measure outcomes.
- How data will be collected.
- How the findings will be reported and used (Hatry et al., 1996).

DECIDING WHAT OUTCOMES TO MEASURE

Determining what outcomes to measure is a logical next step and will serve as a foundation for the entire evaluation process. Therefore, in this early stage, it is important to gather evaluation questions from multiple sources. These questions or the specific outcomes identified should reflect the benefits students will receive as a result of being in the program. Very often key words such as "increased...", "reduced....", "more...", "new...", etc. will be used when writing your program outcomes. Outcomes can be described as initial or short-term in nature (e.g., changes in behavior, skills or attitudes within the first 6 months), intermediate (e.g., changes that occur within 6 to 9 months) or long-term (e.g., meaningful changes in condition or status that are maintained over time). The selection of outcomes can come from any number of methods including a review of the program mission statement, staff discussions or focus groups, discussion with past participants, and collaboration with funders and other programs that serve similar populations.

The development of a program logic model (Hatry et al., 1996) can be very helpful at this point as you attempt to organize and prioritize outcome measures. A logic model is an organizational tool that describes how a program works for the benefit of its participants. It allows one to identify key program elements that must be tracked to assess program effectiveness. Typically, logic models include information about program inputs (i.e., resources needed), activities (i.e., what is done to help students), outputs (i.e., the volume of work that is completed such as the number of counseling sessions held, the number of members who attended group, etc.) and most importantly, outcomes that highlight how participants have benefited from the program.

Logic models are often diagrammed as a sequence of boxes that describe program inputs, activities, outputs and outcomes. The following model (see Figure 8) for an elementary level anger management group serves as an example.

Figure 8 - Sample Logic Model

Program: Elementary Anger Management Group

Inputs:
 Program has one PhD level school psychologist and an MSW clinician, field-tested videos and other teaching materials.

Teachers / parents / special education committees identify children to participate in program.

Activities:
A 10 week, 45-minute group provides direct instruction and support for children who have anger management problems. Activities focus on helping children identify their emotions and learn how to respond safely and appropriately when angry with use of written materials, modeling, videos, role-playing, discussion, stories and homework.

Output:
Eight children are enrolled in the group.

Outcomes:
Initial: Children are knowledgeable about their own anger triggers and signals that indicate increased arousal.
      Children complete weekly assignments.

Intermediate: Children demonstrate new / positive coping strategies during group role plays.
      Children increase number of points earned in milieu.
      Children meet "graduation" requirements for group.
Long-term: Children require fewer class removals or level
      drops for disruptive behavior.

The input that comes from a variety of sources and your work on constructing a program logic model will yield a number of possible outcomes for consideration. The next task is to refine your list by eliminating outcomes that are duplicative, overlapping or simply unimportant. The goal should be on identifying those outcomes – two to four - that best capture the intended benefit(s) for participants.

Hatry et al. (1996) identify three criteria or questions to consider in selecting outcomes. Answering, "yes" to the following questions may help with this task: 1) Can the program influence the outcome in a non-trivial way? 2) Will measurement of the outcome help identify program successes as well as problems or shortcomings? 3) Will others accept this as a valid outcome of the program? Another approach may simply be to ask, "What major activities are we doing now?" and then for each activity, ask, "Why are we doing that?" The answer to this second question is likely to be an outcome. When looking at your list of outcomes it is also important to consider whether the program outputs and short-term, intermediate and long-term outcomes relate logically to each other. In essence, do these relationships reflect the logic of the program and what your inputs, activities and outputs are intended to accomplish?

Once you have developed an initial draft of your program logic model, it is often a good idea to seek feedback from other interested parties or from individuals who may work in similar programs that serve children and youth. Although this may lead to modifications in your original draft of outcomes and require additional planning time, it may be advantageous in the long term because of improved outcome targets and a more broadly supported conceptual foundation.

IDENTIFYING OUTCOME INDICATORS

One of the most challenging activities in program evaluation is deciding what information to collect that will document your program's benefits. More specifically, what criteria and data will be used to measure program outcomes? You will need to select at least one or more indicators for each outcome. Perhaps the most direct method of doing this is to simply list your desired outcomes and then generate a corresponding list of indicators as in the following example.

Figure 9 – Outcome Indicators

Outcome	Indicator(s)
Students attend school regularly. ⟶	- 90% of students have 3 or less absences per quarter.
Students demonstrate improvement in behavioral compliance. ⟶	- % of students who receive a daily rating of 28 or higher per quarter. - Total number of support room referrals per month.

Indicators should always be observable and measurable rather than ambiguous. For example, terms such as "significant," "substantial," and "satisfactory" (e.g., "Students demonstrate substantial reductions in the number of physical restraints.") may indicate improvement but are not specific and remain open to interpretation. Indicators that are operationally defined will leave little, if any, doubt as to what changes or accomplishments occurred. It can be helpful to ask yourself how you will know if the outcome has been achieved. What does it look like? What will you see? How will you know it has happened? Keep refining your query until you believe there is no question that an outcome was reached.

In many cases, an outcome indicator will be a numerical target or statistic (e.g., the number or percentage of students who graduated from the program or received a certain score on a rating scale). These are perhaps the most objective types of indicators and certainly meet the criteria for being specific, measurable and unambiguous. Typically, with program evaluation, data will be collected on individual students but reported as an aggregate accomplishment for all participants. Therefore, as you work to identify your indicators, you will need to consider what statistic will best show your program's accomplishments. Most program indicators are reported in terms of an average number, score or percentage of students reaching a certain criteria (e.g., number or percent of students who maintained a 90% attendance rate or higher over a three-month period). Sophisticated statistical analyses are not necessary particularly if this is your first attempt to conduct a program evaluation and you have limited resources or access to outside measurement expertise.

The United Way document (Hatry et al., 1996) offers a helpful outcome measurement framework that helps guide you through the process of specifying indicators for each desired outcome and then identifying your data sources and data collection methods. Figure 10 illustrates this framework.

Figure 10 - Outcome Measurement Framework

Program: Anger Management

Outcome	Indicator(s)	Data Source	Collection Method
Improved self-control	1. Number of restraints	Staff report	Behavior log
	2. Number of support room referrals	Staff report	Behavior log
	3. Daily points earned	Staff ratings	Daily point card

A key issue that must be addressed in outcome evaluation is whether or not change (i.e., in student behavior, attitudes, knowledge) can be attributed to the program itself. In other words, would changes have occurred in the absence of the program? Demonstrating that changes in behavior are a result of program activities is not always easy because of other factors that may be co-occurring (e.g., change due to students' growth and maturity level, medication adjustments, changes in family status, student contacts with other service providers, time alone and so forth). As much as possible, evaluators need to be alert to potential "outside" influences because critics may otherwise be quick to point these out. Nevertheless, various approaches can be taken to address this issue that range from being fairly simple and inexpensive to highly ambitious and requiring considerable resources.

Probably the most common and simplest approach is to collect data from a group before and at the end of their participation (a pre / post design). The comparison of responses would then provide some evidence for changes in behavior or skills even though it may not be entirely possible to attribute change in outcomes to the program exclusively. One possible option might be to compare the treatment group with some other available "standard" of change that already exists. For example, if one of your program indicators is the number of student dropouts per year in grades 10, 11, and 12, there may be local, state or national trend data available that reports student dropout rates for students in these grades. A comparison of these figures could then be helpful in determining how effective your program is in reducing student dropout rates. Obviously, when making such comparisons, you would need to establish to at least some extent that the two groups are comparable to begin with. Otherwise, if your particular group of students is not "typical" of other students in the state, comparisons would be inappropriate.

A more rigorous method for evaluating outcomes is to compare the performance of those who receive the treatment with a similar group of students (i.e., a control group) who do not receive the treatment. This represents one of the most straightforward methods of determining program effectiveness. Another method of comparing groups - using a multiple baseline design - is to divide students into several groups and stagger the initiation of treatment, with one group receiving intervention in the initial offering and other groups in subsequent offerings. Essentially, those students in the first group become the treatment group and students in subsequent groups become the comparison group. This may be a very useful strategy to use especially when a program is unable to provide services to students at one time or when not all students are required to receive the intervention. Again, as with any experimental or quasi-experimental design, it would be important to insure that staggered groups are comparable in terms of a number of student variables (e.g., age, gender, race,

IQ, test scores, etc.). If groups are similar to begin with, you can be more confident that any post-treatment differences between groups are more likely to be a result of the program.

METHODS TO COLLECT INFORMATION

Once you have identified what information is needed to document improvement, you will need to determine how best to collect that information. There are multiple methods for collecting data and each has its own advantages and disadvantages. The most common methods include use of questionnaires, checklists, surveys, interviews, observations, documentation reviews (e.g., behavior logs, attendance records, test scores, etc.), ratings by trained observers and case studies.

Program evaluators must determine whether they will need to design their own instruments for evaluating program implementation and outcomes or use pre-existing methods and measures. This will obviously depend on the specific goals of the program and those questions you wish to answer. Because of the unique characteristics of many therapeutic, educational and special intervention programs, it may be necessary to develop your own measures. Information that is specific to instrument design for applied research can be found in a number of helpful resources (U.S. General Accounting Office, 1993; Fink, 1995; Hatry et al., 1996; Herman, 1991; Rossi & Freeman, 1987; Sudman & Bradburn, 1982).

While the development of your own data collection instruments may best suit your needs, there are several advantages of using published instruments that should also be considered. First, would be the obvious benefits with respect to the amount of time and effort that would be saved when having to design and pilot your own measurement instrument (i.e., questionnaire, survey, interview format, etc.). Second, pre-existing measures have typically established reliability and validity for their items that can increase the power of your findings and there is often the availability of other comparison groups. A possible disadvantage may involve cost due to copyright provisions of the instrument. One would also need to insure that the instrument adequately addresses the evaluation's concerns and that the comparison group (i.e., the instrument's population sample) is comparable to the group you are studying.

Certainly, a primary goal in selecting any evaluation method is to obtain the most relevant and useful data in the most cost-effective and efficient manner. In an effort to accomplish this, McNamara (1999) suggests that evaluators consider the following questions:

1. What specific information is needed to make decisions about a program?
2. How much of this information can be collected and analyzed in a cost-effective manner?
3. Will the methods be sufficient to collect needed information?
4. Will the information appear credible to others?
5. Will participants respond meaningfully or carefully? (e.g., when completing questionnaires, surveys, etc.).
6. Who can administer the evaluation methods? Is training required?
7. How can the information be analyzed and best presented?

Ideally, information should be collected from a variety of sources using a combination of methods. Questionnaires and documentation reviews can provide a great deal of information in a relatively short period of time while interviews and case studies can be used for more in-depth analysis. It may be helpful at this stage to simply write a brief procedure that specifies what data will be collected, how it will be collected, who will collect it, when it will be collected and what specifically will be done with the data?

Finally, when developing any data collection method, there are certain procedural issues that should be considered. Perhaps the most important among these include the following:

- When should data be collected? At the start or end of the program? At specific time intervals?
- Who would be considered a participant? Only those who completed the program? Those who dropped out? Those who refused or were ineligible?
- Will all participants be included or only a sample?
- Who will collect the data? Will data collectors need to be trained?
- How will confidentiality be protected?

- How will your participants be informed about the data collection process? (Hatry et al., 1996)

ANALYZING AND REPORTING OUTCOMES
Data Analysis

Following your data collection efforts, you will need to organize data in a manner that facilitates analysis and understanding. Generally this means transferring quantitative data from questionnaires, surveys, interview sheets and other documents onto a simple (e.g., manual) spreadsheet or computer file. There are a number of easy-to-use spreadsheet or database software programs available for data entry and analysis (e.g., *Excel, Lotus 1-2-3, Corel Quattro Pro, IPASS Program*). However, it is most likely that you will not need to use sophisticated statistical analyses.

Once information is transferred to your summary sheet or spreadsheet, data can then be tabulated to yield the desired calculation or numerical representation you want to report. For example, your basic data may include:

- Total number of students completing the program.
- Percent of students achieving each outcome status.
- Average or median scores on a certain measure.
- Frequency of specific interventions required.

It may also be important to analyze your data from the perspective of key characteristics of program participants. For example, are there any differences in outcome noted between males and females, younger or older students, time spent in program, severity of disability, degree of parent support, etc?

In addition to quantitative data, qualitative data can yield valuable information. Because of the more open-ended format, you may be more likely to obtain new or serendipitous information that conveys specific concerns, themes or recommendations for the program. To analyze this type of information, it may be helpful to organize respondent comments into categories that could be labeled as concerns, strengths, weaknesses, recommendations, etc. Categorizing this information can make it easier to identify patterns or causal relationships in themes (e.g., students who served as "peer helpers" had the fewest support room referrals).

PRESENTING YOUR DATA

The report of evaluation findings will not only include reference to your data but also offer explanations to help readers understand what the numbers mean. This will enable your audience to gain a more thorough understanding of what the program is trying to accomplish. A discussion of results can provide program investigators the opportunity to state probable reasons for certain outcomes. This could be especially important if your outcomes are particularly low, high or otherwise very different from what you expected. In the event that your results are worse than expected, the discussion may focus on recommendations for change in order to improve in the future.

Outcome data that is converted to visual presentations can often make results more understandable to readers. For example, data tables can summarize numerical data effectively by grouping pertinent information together. Figure 11 is an example of a data table reporting data for one outcome of the Broad Street Behavioral Skills program.

Figure 11 – Behavioral Skills Program:
 # Support Room Referrals

Ages:	5-6	7-8	9-10	11-12	13-14	Total
Sept-Oct	22	25	49	60	55	211
May-June	15	10	39	65	30	159

Bar graphs can also be effective in showing distributions of discrete or categorical data in reference to some unit of measurement (e.g., number or percentage for whom an outcome occurred). Figure 12 provides an example of a bar graph that shows the number of physical restraints given during the school year.

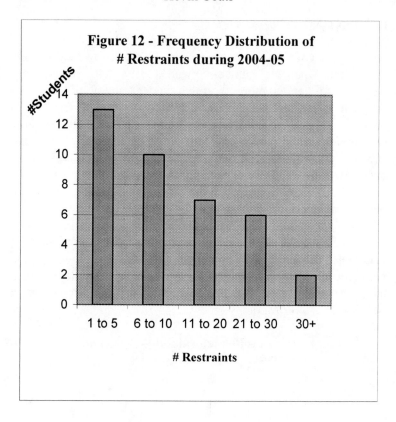

Figure 12 - Frequency Distribution of
Restraints during 2004-05

The use of pie charts is another relatively common method of illustrating the distribution of a given indicator, with each percentage being represented by a slice of the total pie. For example, Figure 13 provides a visual display of student placement outcomes for the year.

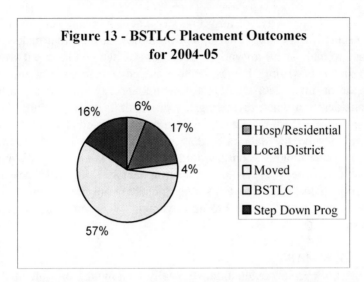

**Figure 13 - BSTLC Placement Outcomes
for 2004-05**

Hosp/Residential
Local District
Moved
BSTLC
Step Down Prog

Although certain agencies or funding sources may require a written report that follows a predetermined format, many do not. However, most evaluation reports contain pertinent information that is organized in a manner that tells about the program and its goals as well as the evaluation methodology, results, interpretations, recommendations and, possibly, an action plan. McNamara (1998) suggests the following format for an evaluation report:

- Title page (with name of program or organization, date)
- Table of contents
- Executive summary (e.g., a one-page summary of findings/recommendations)
- Background and overall goal of the program
- Overall evaluation goal(s) – What questions are being answered by the evaluation?
- Evaluation methodology – type of data collected, instruments or methods used, how data was analyzed, limitations of the evaluation methods
- Interpretations and conclusions
- Recommendations
- Appendices (e.g., instruments used, testimonials from participants, related literature).

The essence of any report is whether or not your data is presented in a clear, concise, and organized fashion that makes it easy to understand for various audiences. Once you have put your findings in writing, it may be to your advantage to seek others input or impressions. The following are key questions worth consideration when reviewing the initial draft of any report: Do the findings seem reasonable? Is the data presented clearly? What questions do the data raise that are not included in the report? What other tables or charts would be helpful? Is anything missing that might be seen as an influencing factor? Any feedback in response to these questions may not only improve your final evaluation report but lead to improvement with your measurement system.

SUMMARY

Program evaluation, typically following an outcomes-based model, is often seen as an essential component in most human service and educational programs. Aside from the importance of establishing accountability for use of resources, a more fundamental purpose of evaluation is to determine whether the program makes a difference for the people it serves. Ideally, the process of evaluation should be viewed as an integrated and ongoing activity rather than an event that stands alone. Similarly, it does not need to be a highly complex process requiring advanced statistical analyses or expertise other than the requirement that program evaluators use valid and reliable measures.

Evaluation is viewed as a systematic and highly organized set of activities that begin with a clear understanding of purpose as well as the identification of desired program outcomes and indicators. Fortunately, there are many resources available that can serve as a helpful guide for measuring outcomes and using the results effectively.

APPENDIX A

Recommended Resources

AFT – American Federation of Teachers
555 New Jersey Avenue, NW, Washington, DC 20001
(p) 202-897-4400
www.aft.org

American Psychological Association
750 First Street, NE, Washington, DC 20002-4242
(p) 202-336-5500 (f) 202-336-5502
www.apa.org

ASPIRE – Associations of Service Providers Implementing IDEA
Reforms in Education
Council for Exceptional Children
1110 North Glebe Road, Suite 300, Arlington, VA 22201-5704
(p) 877-CEC-IDEA (TDD) 866-915-5000 (f) 703-264-1637
www.ideapractices.org

CASEL – Collaborative to Advance Social and Emotional
Learning
Department of Psychology – University of Illinois at Chicago
1007 West Harrison Street, Chicago, IL 60607-7137
(p) 312-413-1008 (f) 312-355-4480
www.CASEL.org

Center for Effective Collaboration and Practice
American Institutes for Research
1000 Thomas Jefferson Street, NW, Washington, DC 20007
(p) 888-457-1551 (TDD) 877-334-3499 (f) 202-944-5454
www.air.org/cecp/

Center for Mental Health in Schools
Department of Psychology
P.O. Box 951563
Los Angeles, CA 90095-1563
(p) 310-825-3634 (f) 310-206-8716
http://smhp.psych.ucla.edu

Center for the Prevention of School Violence
313 Chapanoke Road, Suite 140, Raleigh, NC 27603
(p) 800-299-6054 (f) 919-773-2904
www.ncsu.edu/cpsv/

Counseling and Student Services Clearinghouse
ERIC – Education Resource Information Center
201 Ferguson Building, P.O. Box 26171, Greensboro, NC 27402-6171
(p) 800-414-9769 (f) 336-334-4116
http://ericcass.uncg.edu

Girls and Boys Town – National Resource & Training Center
Father Flanagan's Boys' Home
14100 Crawford Street
Boys Town, NE 68010
www.girlsandboystown.org/nrtc

KidsPeace – National Centers
5300 KidsPeace Drive
Orefield, PA 18669
1-800-8KID-123

NASP – National Association of School Psychologists
4340 East West Highway, Suite 402, Bethesda, MD 20814
(p) 301-657-0270 (f) 301-657-0275
www.nasponline.org

NEA – National Education Association
1201 16th Street, NW, Washington, DC 20036
(p) 202-833-4000 (f) 202-822-7482
www.nea.org

National Institute on the Education of At-Risk Students
U.S. Department of Education
OERI/At-Risk, Room 610, 555New Jersey Ave., NW,
Washington, DC 20208-5521
(p) 202-219-2239 (f) 202-210-2030
www.ed.gov/offices/OERI/At-Risk/

National Mental Health and Education Center
National Association of School Psychologists
4340 East West Highway, Suite 402, Bethesda, MD 20814
(p) 301-657-0270 (f) 301-657-0275
www.naspcenter.org

National Resource Center for Safe Schools
101 SW Main Street, Suite 500, Portland, OR 97204
(p) 800-268-2275 (f) 503-275-0444
www.safetyzone.org

Positive Behavioral Interventions and Supports
5262 University of Oregon, Eugene, OR 97403-5262
(p) 541-346-2505 (f) 541-346-5689
www.pbis.org

Safe and Drug Free Schools Program
400 Maryland Avenue, SW, Room 3E314, Washington, DC
20002
(p) 202-260-3954 (f) 202-260-7767
www.ed.gov/offices/OESE/SDFS/

REFERENCES

Adams, G. L. & Engelmann, S. (1996). *Research on direct instruction: 25 years beyond DISTAR.* Seattle, WA: Educational Achievement Systems.

Adelman, H. & Taylor, L. (1999). Mental health in schools and systems restructuring. *Clinical Psychology Review, 19,* 137-163.

Adelman, H. & Taylor, L. (1993). School-based mental health: Toward a comprehensive approach. *Journal of Mental Health Administration, 20,* 32-45.

Algozzine, R. , Schmid, R. & Mercer, C.D. (1981). *Childhood behavior disorders: Applied research and educational practice.* Rockville, MD: Aspen.

Atkins, M. S., Graczyk, P. A., Frazier, S. L. & Abdul-Adil, J. (2003). Toward a new model for promoting urban children's mental health: Accessible, effective and sustainable school-based mental health services. *School Psychology Review, 32* (4), 503-514.

Axelrod, S. & Apsche, J. (1982). *The effects of punishment on human behavior.* New York: Academic Press.

Ayllon, T. & Azrin, N. (1968). *The token economy: A motivational system for therapy and rehabilitation.* New York: Appleton-Century-Crofts.

Ayllon, T. & Michael, J. (1959). The psychiatric nurse as a behavior engineer. *Journal of the Experimental Analysis of Behavior, 2,* 323-334.

Azrin, N. & Holtz, W. (1966). Punishment. In W. K. Honig (Ed.), *Operant behavior: Areas of research and application.* New York: Appelton-Century-Crofts.

Ball, A. (1997). The Dallas County Juvenile Justice Alternative Education System. *Reaching Today's Youth, 1* (2), 63-64.

Bandura, A. (1973). *Aggression: A social learning analysis.* Engelwood Cliffs, NJ: Prentice-Hall.

Bandura, A. (1978). The self system in reciprocal determination. *American Psychologist, 33,* 344-358.

Barrish, H., Saunders, M. & Wolf, M. (1969). Good behavior game: Effects of individual contingencies for group consequences on disruptive behavior in the classroom. *Journal of Applied Behavior Analysis, 2,* 119-124.

Bear, G. G., Quinn, M. M. & Burkholder, S. (2001). *Interim alternative educational settings for children with disabilities.* Bethesda, MD: National Association of School Psychologists.

Bear, G. G., Webster-Stratton, C., Furlong, M. & Rhee, S. (2000). Preventing aggression and violence. In K. M. Minke & G. G.

Bear (Eds.), *Preventing school problems – promoting school success: Strategies and programs that work* (pp. 1-69). Bethesda, MD: National Association of School Psychologists.

Behling, D. (1994). School uniforms and person perception. *Perceptual and Motor Skills, 79,* 723-729.

Berg, I. K. & Steiner, T. (2003). *Children's solution work.* New York: W. W. Norton and Company.

Bishop, G., Rosen, L., Miller, C. & Hendrickson, J. (1996). Evaluation of the Boys Town motivation system in a U. S. school setting. *School Psychology International, 17,* 125-131.

Blackwood, R. (1970). The operant conditioning of verbally mediated self-control in the classroom. *Journal of School Psychology, 8,* 251-258.

Bleckman, E. A., Prinz, R. J., Dumas, J. E. (1995). Coping, competence and aggression prevention: Part 1. developmental model. *Applied and Preventive Psychology, 4,* 211-232.

Bloomquist, M. L. (1996). *Skills training for children with behavior disorders.* New York: Guilford Press.

Bowditch, C. (1993). Getting rid of troublemakers: High school disciplinary procedures and the production of dropouts. *Social Problems, 40,* 493-507.

Bridge, B., Gallagher, M., Livermon, B., Nusbaum, R. & Bierman, B. (1986). *Coolaid: How to manage seriously disruptive behaviors.* Baltimore, MD: The Children's Guild, Inc.

Brooks, R. (1991). *The self-esteem teacher.* Loveland, OH: Treehaus Communications, Inc.

Brooks, R. & Goldstein, S. (2001). *Raising resilient children: Fostering strength, hope and optimism in your child.* Chicago: Contemporary Books.

Calfee, C., Wittwer, F. & Meredith, M. (1998). *Building a full-service school: A step-by-step guide.* San Francisco: Jossey-Bass.

CALM Training Services, Ltd. (1997). Clackmannanshire, Scotland.

Camp, B. (1977). Verbal mediation in young aggressive boys. *Journal of Abnormal Psychology, 86,* 145-153.

Camp, B. & Bash, M. (1981). *Think aloud: Increasing social and cognitive skills – A problem solving program for children.* Champaign, IL: Research Press.

Caraulia, A. P. & Steiger, L.K. (1997). *Nonviolent crisis intervention: Learning to defuse explosive behavior.* Brookfield, WI: CPI Publishing.

Carlson, C. D. & Francis, D. J. (2002). Increasing the reading achievement of at-risk children through direct instruction: Evaluation of the Rodeo Institute for Teacher Excellence

(RITE). *Journal of Education for Students Placed at Risk, 7* (2), 141-166.

Center for Effective Collaboration & Practice. (1998). *Addressing student problem behavior: An IEP team's introduction to functional behavioral assessment and intervention plan.* American Institute for Research. Washington, D. C. Retrieved May 9, 2004, from www.airdc.org/cecp/resources/problem behavior/conducting.html.

Centers for Disease Control National Center for Injury Control & Prevention (1996). *Ten leading causes of death, United States, 1996.* Atlanta, Georgia: U.S. department of Health & Human Services.

Center for Mental Health in Schools. (1999). *Conduct and behavior problems: Intervention and resources for school aged youth.* Retrieved June 13, 2004, from http://smhp.psych.ucla.edu.

Center for Mental Health in Schools. (2000). *Financial strategies to aid in addressing barriers to learning.* Available: http//smhp.psych.ucla.edu/pdfdocs/financial/fund2000.pdf

Chalfant, J. C., Pysh, M. X. & Moultrie, R. (1979). Teacher assistance teams: A model for within building problem solving. *Learning Disabilities Quarterly, 2,* 85-96.

Chandler, K. A., Chapman, C. D., Rand, M. R. & Taylor, B. M. (1998). *Student's reports of school crime: 1989 & 1995* (NCES Report 98-241). Washington, D. C.: U.S. Departments of Education and Justice.

Coats, K. I. (2002). *Annual Report on Student Behavioral Outcomes: BSTLC.* Unpublished document, WSWHE BOCES, Hudson Falls, NY.

Coats, K. I. (2001). *Behavior management guidelines: Broad Street Teaching & Learning Center.* Hudson Falls, NY: WSWHE BOCES Print Shop.

Coats, K. I. (1979). Cognitive self-instructional training approach for reducing disruptive behavior of young children. *Psychological Reports, 44,* 127-134.

Cohen, J. J. & Fish, M. C. (1993). *Handbook of school-based interventions: Resolving student problems and promoting healthy educational environments.* New York: Jossey-Bass.

Collaborative to Advance Social and Emotional Learning (CASEL). (2000). *Social and emotional learning competencies.* Retrieved April 2, 2004, from http://www.casel.org/competencies.htm.

Collins, M. (n.d.). *Using software systems to measure nonprofit program outcomes: Assessing the benefits and barriers for strategic management.* Retrieved July 9, 2005 from http://pages.prodigy.net/michael_collins/Outcomes_IT.doc

Colvin, G. & Fernandez, E. (2000). Sustaining effective behavior support systems in an elementary school. *Journal of Positive Behavior Interventions, 2* (4), 251-254.

Connolly, T., Dowd, T., Criste, A., Nelson, C. & Tobias, L. (1995). *The well- managed classroom: Promoting student success through social skill instruction.* Father Flanagan's Boys' Home, Boys Town, NE: Boys Town Press.

Costenbader, V. K. & Markson, S. (1994). School suspension: A survey of current policies and practices. *NASSP Bulletin, 78,* 103-107.

Council of Administrators of Special Education. (1994). CASE position paper on delivery of services to students with disabilities. (Available from Council for Exceptional Children, Reston, VA).

Council for Exceptional Children. (1993). *CEC policy on inclusive schools and community settings.* Reston, VA: Author.

Council for Exceptional Children. (1997). Emerging models. *Research Connections* (Fall). Retrieved May 15, 2004, from http://www.cec.sped.org/osep/art2.html.

Cox, S. M., Davidson, W. S. & Bynum, T. S. (1995). A meta-analytic assessment of delinquency-related outcomes of alternative education programs. *Crime and Delinquency, 41,* 219-234.

Crews, G. A. & Counts, M. R. (1997). *The evaluation of school disturbance in America: Colonial times to modern day.* Westport, CT: Praeger.

Crone, D. A. & Horner, R. H. (2003). *Building positive behavioral support systems in schools: Functional behavioral assessment.* New York: Guilford Press.

Curtis, M. J., Curtis, V. A. & Graden, J. L. (1988). Prevention and early intervention through intervention assistance programs. *School Psychology International, 9,* 257-264.

Curtis, M. J., Zuns, J. E. & Graden, J. L. (1987). Pre-referral intervention programs: Enhancing student performance in regular education settings. In C. A. Maher & J. E. Zins (Eds.), *Psychoeducational interventions in the schools: Methods and procedures for enhancing student competence* (pp 7-25). Elmsford, New York: Pergamon Press.

Daly, P. & Ranalli, P. (2003). Using countoons to teach self-monitoring skills. *Teaching Exceptional Children, 35* (5), 30-35.

Darveaux, D. X. (1984). The good behavior game plus merit: Controlling disruptive behavior and improving student motivation. *School Psychology Review, 13,* 510-514.

Dowd, T. & Tierney, J. (1992). *Teaching social skills to youth.* Boys Town, NE: The Boys Town Press.

DeRisi, W. J. & Butz, G. (1975). *Writing behavioral contracts: A case simulation practice manual.* Champaign, IL: Research Press.

Dickson, L., Thompson, R. & Swan, B. (1999). *A longitudinal study of students with SE/BD using the Boys Town teaching model.* Paper presented at the International Council for Children with Behavioral Disorders, Dallas, TX.

Dowd, T., Tobias, L., Connolly, T., Criste, A. & Nelson, C. (1993). *Specialized classroom management: A Boys Town approach.* Boys Town, NE: The Boys Town Press.

Duke, D. (1989). School organization, leadership and student behavior. In O. C. Moles (Ed.), *Strategies to reduce student misbehavior.* Washington, D. C.: Office of Educational Research and Improvement, U. S. Department of Education.

DuPaul, G. (2003). Commentary: Bridging the gap between research and practice. *School Psychology Review, 32* (2), 178-180.

Dupper, D. & Krishef, C. (1993). School-based social-cognitive skills training for middle school students with school behavior problems. *Children and Youth Services Review, 15,* 131-142.

Duppong Hurley, K. & Hyland, T. (2000). Girls and Boys Town education model shows promise with elementary and adolescent SE/BD students. *Teaching Family Association Newsletter,* Teaching Family Association, 910 Charles Street, Fredericksburg, VA 22401.

Dryfoos, J. G. (1994). *Full service schools.* San Francisco: Jossey-Bass.

Dryfoos, J. G. & Maguire, S. (2002). *Inside full service community schools.* Thousand Oaks, CA: Corwin Press.

Dwyer, K. P. & Gorin, S. (1996). A national perspective of school psychology in the context of school reform. *School Psychology Review, 25,* 507-511.

Dwyer, K. P. & Osher, D. (2000). *Safeguarding our children: An action guide.* Washington, D. C.: U. S. Departments of Education and Justice, American Institutes for Research.

Dwyer, K. P., Osher, D. & Warger, C. (1998). *Early warning, timely response: A guide to safe schools.* Washington, D. C.: U. S. Department of Education.

Eber, L. (1997). Improving school-based behavioral interventions through use of the wraparound process. *Reaching Today's Youth, 1* (2), 32-36.

Engelmann, S., Becker, W. C.& Gersten, R. (1988). The direct instruction follow through model: Design and outcomes. *Education and Treatment of Children, 11* (4), 303-317.

Evans, C. (2002). Administrative sanctions, classroom management and intervention strategies: Building blocks for school-wide discipline. CASE/CCBD Mini-Library Series: *Safe, drug-free and effective schools*, Arlington, VA: The CEC.

Everly, G., Flannery, R. & Mitchell, J. (in press). CISM: A review of literature. *Aggression and Violent Behavior: A Review Journal.*

Everly, G. & Mitchell, J. (1997). *Critical incident stress management (CISM): A new era and standard of care in crisis intervention.* Ellicot City, MD: Chevron.

Ewing, T. (2000). Time-out: Guidelines for teachers. *Behavioral interventions: Creating a safe environment in our schools.* National Mental Health and Education Center for Children and Families. Bethesda, MD: National Association of School Psychologists.

Ferferman, F. (n.d.). Software for handling your quantitative data. *Star Systems Tech Talk.* Retrieved June 5, 2005, from http://www.os.dhhs.gov.

Feindler, E., Marriott, S. & Iwata, M. (1984). Group anger control training for junior high school delinquents. *Cognitive Therapy and Research, 8*, 3, 299-311.

Fetterman, D. (2001). *Foundations of empowerment evaluation.* Thousand Oaks, CA: Sage Publications.

Fetterman, D., Kafterian, S. & Wandersman, A. (1996). *Empowerment evaluation: Knowledge and tools for self-assessment and accountability.* Thousand Oaks, CA: Sage Publications.

Fink, A. (1995). *The survey kit.* Thousand Oaks, CA: Sage Publications.

Fish, M. C. & Mendola, L. R. (1986). The effect of self-instruction training on homework completion in an elementary special education class. *School Psychology Review, 15*, 268-276.

Forman, S. (1980). A comparison of cognitive training and response cost procedures in modifying aggressive behavior of elementary school children. *Behavior Therapy, 11*, 594-600.

Forehand, R. & Wierson, M. (1993). The role of developmental factors in planning behavioral interventions for children: Disruptive behavior as an example. *Behavior Therapy, 24*, 117-141.

Foster-Johnson, L. & Dunlap, G. (1993). Using functional assessment to develop effective, individualized interventions. *Teaching Exceptional Children, 25*, 44-50.

Foxx, R. & Azrin, N. (1972). Restitution: A method of eliminating aggressive-disruptive behavior of retarded and brain damaged patients. *Behavior Research and Therapy, 10*, 15-27.

Foxx, R. & Bechtel, D. (1983). Overcorrection: A review and analysis. In S. Axelrod and J. Apache (Eds.), *The effects of punishment on human behavior.* New York: Academic Press.

Foxx, C., Foxx, R., Jones, J. & Kiely, D. (1980). Twenty-four hour social isolation. *Behavior Modification, 4*, 130-144.

Gagne, R. (1965). *The conditions of learning.* New York: Holt, Rinehart & Winston.

Gast, D. & Nelson, C. (1977). Legal and ethical considerations for the use of time out in special education settings. *Journal of Special Education, 11*, 457-467.

Gaustad, J. (1992). *School discipline.* ERIC Digest 78, ERIC Clearinghouse on Educational Management.

Gettinger, M. (1985). Effects of teacher-directed versus student-directed instruction and cues versus no cues for improving spelling performance. *Journal of Applied Behavior Analysis, 18*, 167-171.

Glasser, W. (1990). *The quality school: Managing students without coercion.* New York: Harper Collins Publishers, Inc.

Goldstein, A. P. (1988). *The prepare curriculum: Teaching prosocial competencies.* Champaign, IL: Research Press.

Goldstein, A. P. & Glick, B. (1987). *Aggression replacement training: A comprehensive intervention for aggressive youth.* Champaign, IL: Research Press.

Goldstein, A. P., Sprafkin, R. P., Gershaw, N. J. & Klein, P. (1980). *Skillstreaming the adolescent: A structured learning approach to teaching prosocial skills.* Champaign, IL: Research Press.

Good, J. E. & Brophy, T. L. (1994). *Looking in classrooms.* New York: Longman.

Gordon, M. (1979). The assessment of impulsivity and mediating behaviors in hyperactive and non-hyperactive boys. *Journal of Abnormal Child Psychology, 7*, 317-326.

Gottfredson, D. G. (1989). Developing effective organizations to reduce school disorder. In O. C. Moles (Ed.), *Strategies to reduce student misbehavior.* Washington, D. C.: Office of Educational Research and Improvement (ERIC Document Reproduction Service No. ED 311 608).

Graden, J. L., Casey, A. & Christenson, S.L. (1985). Implementing a pre-referral intervention system: Part I. the model. *Exceptional Children, 51*, 377-384.

Graybill, D., Jamison, M. & Swerdlik, M. (1984). Remediation of impulsivity in learning disabled children by special education resource teachers using verbal self-instruction. *Psychology in the Schools, 21*, 252-254.

Gresham, F. M. & Lambros, K. M. (1998). Behavioral and functional assessment. In T. S. Watson & F. M. Gresham (Eds.), *Handbook of child behavior therapy* (pp. 3-22). New York: Plenum Press.

Gresham, F. M., Watson, T. S. & Skinner, C. H. (2001). Functional behavioral assessment: Principles, procedures and future directions. *School Psychology Review*, *30* (2), 156-172.

Grosenick, J. K., George, N. L., George, M. P. & Lewis, T. J. (1991). Public school services for behavioral disordered students: Program practices in the 1980s. *Behavioral Disorders*, *16*, 87-96.

Guerra, N. & Slaby, R. (1990). Cognitive mediators of aggression in adolescent offenders: 2. Intervention. *Journal of Developmental Psychology*, *26* (2), 269-277.

Gumpel, T. & Shlomit, D. (2000). Exploring the efficacy of self-regulatory training as a possible alternative to social skills training. *Behavioral Disorders*, *25*, 131-141.

Hall, R., Axelrod, S., Foundopoulos, M., Shellman, J., Campbell, R. & Cranston, S. (1971). The effective use of punishment to modify behavior in the classroom. *Educational Technology*, *11*, 24-26.

Halpern, R. (1990). Poverty and early childhood parenting: Toward a framework for intervention. *American Journal of Orthopsychiatry*, *60*, 6-18.

Halpren, A. S. & Fuhrer, M. J. (Eds.) (1984). *Functional assessment in rehabilitation*. Baltimore: Paul H. Brooks.

Hampton, L. (1999). *Satori alternatives to managing aggression*. SanAntonio, TX: Satori Learning Designs, Inc.

Harris, V. & Sherman, J. (1973). Use and analysis of the "good behavior game" to reduce disruptive classroom behavior. *Journal of Applied Behavior Analysis*, *6*, 405-417.

Heaviside, S., Rowand, C., Williams, C. & Farris, E. (1998). *Violence and discipline problems in U.S. public schools: 1996-97* (NCES 98-030). Washington, D.C.: U.S. Department of Education, National Center for Education Statistics.

Herman, J. (Ed.) (1991). *Program evaluation kit*. Thousand Oaks, CA: Sage Publications.

Horner, R. H., Dunlap, G., Koegel, R., Carr, E., Sailor, W., Anderson, J., Albin, R. & O'Neill, R. (1990). In support of integration for people with severe problem behaviors: A response to four commentaries. *Journal of the Association for Persons with Severe Handicaps*, *15*, 145-147.

Hyman, I. & Perone, D. (1998). The other side of school violence: Educator policies and practices that may contribute to student misbehavior. *Journal of School Psychology*, *30*, 7-27.

Idol, L., Paolucci-Whitcomb, P. & Nevin, A. (1993). *Collaborative consultation*. Austin, TX: Pro-Ed.

Imich, A. (1994). Exclusions from school: Current trends and issues. *Educational Research*, *36* (1), 3-11.

Individuals with Disabilities Act Amendments of 1997, 20 U. S. C. 1400 et seq.

Jenkins, P. H. (1997). School delinquency and the school social bond. *Journal of Research in Crime and Delinquency, 34*, 337-367.

Jones, F. & Miller, W. (1974). The effective use of negative attention for reducing group disruption in special elementary school classrooms. *The Psychological Record, 24*, 435-448.

Kaplan, J. S. (2000). *Beyond functional assessment*. New York: Pro-Ed.

Kanfer, F. (1970). Self-monitoring: Methodological issues and clinical applications. *Journal of Consulting and Clinical Psychology, 35*, 143-152.

Kaufman, K. & O'Leary, K. (1972). Reward, cost and self-evaluation procedures for disruptive adolescents in a psychiatric hospital school. *Journal of Applied Behavior Analysis, 5*, 293-310.

Kazdin, A. (1980). Acceptability of alternative treatments for deviant child behavior. *Journal of Applied Behavior Analysis, 13*, 259-273.

Kendall, P. & Braswell, L. (1985). *Cognitive-behavioral therapy for impulsive children*. New York: Guilford.

Kunzelmann, H., Cohen, M., Hulten, W., Martin, G. & Mingo, A. (1970). *Precision teaching: An initial training sequence*. Seattle, WA: Special Child Publications.

Lewis, T. & Sugai, G. (1999). Effective behavior support: A systems approach to proactive school-wide management. *Focus on Exceptionalities, 31* (6), 1-24.

Liontos, L. B. (1991). *Involving at-risk families in their children's education* (ERIC Digest Series Number EA58). [Electronic version]. Eugene, OR: ERIC Clearinghouse on Educational Management. (ERIC Document Reproduction Service Number ED326925).

Lloyd, J., Landrum, T. & Hallahan, D. (1991). Self-monitoring applications for classroom intervention. In G. Stoner, M. Shinn & H. Walker (Eds.), *Interventions for achievement and behavior problems*. Silver Spring, MD: National Association of School Psychologists.

Lochman, J., Burch, P., Curry, J. & Lampron, L (1984). Treatment and generalization effects of cognitive-behavioral and goal-setting interventions with aggressive boys. *Journal of Consulting and Clinical Psychology, 52* (5), 915-916.

Lochman, J. & Lenhart, L. (1993). Anger coping intervention for aggressive children: conceptual models and outcome effects. *Clinical Psychology Review, 13*, 785-805.

Lochman, J. & Wells, K. (1996). A social-cognitive intervention with aggressive children. In D. Peters & R. McMahon (Eds.), *Preventing childhood disorders, substance abuse and delinquency*. Thousand Oaks, CA: Sage Publications, 111-143.

Loeber, R. & Farrington, D. (1998). *Serious and violent juvenile offenders: Risk factors and successful interventions*. Thousand Oaks, CA: Sage Publications.

Lovaas, O., Koegel, R., Simmons, J. & Long, J. (1973). Some generalization and follow-up measures on autistic children in behavior therapy. *Journal of Applied Behavior Analysis, 6*, 131-166.

Luria, A. (1961). *The role of speech in the regulation of normal and abnormal behavior*. New York: Liveright.

MacMillan, D., Gresham, F. & Forness, S. (1996). Full inclusion: An empirical perspective. *Behavioral Disorders, 21*, 145-159.

MacPherson, E., Candee, B. & Hohman, R. (1974). A comparison of three methods for eliminating disruptive lunchroom behavior. *Journal of Applied Behavior Analysis, 7*, 287-297.

Madsen, C., Becker, W. & Thomas, D. (1968). Rules, praise and ignoring: Elements of elementary classroom control. *Journal of Applied Behavior Analysis, 1*, 139-150.

McDougall, D. (1998). Research on self-management techniques used by students with disabilities in general education settings: A descriptive review. *Remedial and Special Education, 19*, 310-320.

McDougall, D. & Brady, M. (1998). Initiating and fading self-management interventions to increase math fluency in general education classes. *Exceptional Children, 64*, 151-166.

McNamara, C. (1998). *Basic guide to program evaluation*. Retrieved October 10, 2005, from http://www.managementhelp.org/evaluatn/fnl_eval.htm

Mannix, D. (1993). *Social skills activities for special children*. West Nyack, NY: The Center for Applied Research in Education.

Mayer, G. (1995). Preventing anti-social behavior in the schools. *Journal of Applied Behavior Analysis, 4*.

McDonnell, C. & Barren, K. (1994). What's happening to our children? *Maryland Bar Journal, 27*.

McGinnis, E. & Goldstein, A. (1984). *Skillstreaming the elementary school child: A guide for teaching prosocial skills*. Champaign, IL: Research Press.

McLaughlin, T. F. (1976). Self-control in the classroom. *Review of Educational Research, 46*, 631-663.

Meichenbaum, D. & Goodman, J. (1969). The developmental control of operant motor responding by verbal operants. *Journal of Experimental Child Psychology, 7*, 553-565.

Meichenbaum, D. & Goodman, J. (1971). Training impulsive children to talk to themselves: A means of developing self-control. *Journal of Consulting and Clinical Psychology, 40,* 148-154.

Minke, K. & Bear, G. (2000). *Preventing school problems – promoting school success: Strategies and programs that work.* Bethesda, MD: National Association of School Psychologists.

Morgan-D'Atrio, C., Northrup, J., LaFleur, L. & Spera, S. (1996). Toward prescriptive alternatives to suspensions: A preliminary evaluation. *Behavioral Disorders, 21,* 190-200.

Murray, R. K. (1997). The impact of school uniforms on school climate. *NASSP Bulletin, 81* (593), 106-112.

Myers, V. & Lkine, C. (2001). Secondary school intervention assistance teams: Can they be effective? *The High School Journal, 85* (2), 33-43.

Nastasi, B., Varjas, K. & Bernstein, R. (1998). *Exemplary mental health programs: School psychologists as mental health service providers.* Washington, D. C.: National Association of School Psychologists.

National Association of School Psychologists. (1986). *Intervention assistance teams: A model for building level instructional problem-solving.* Silver spring, MD: Author.

National Association of School Psychologists. (2001). *Positive behavioral supports, zero tolerance, fair discipline – fact sheets.* Retrieved June 12, 2004, from http://www.nasponline.org

National Association of State Boards of Education. (1992). *Winners all: A call for inclusive schools.* Retrieved March 5, 2004, from http://www.nasbe.org/Educational_Issues/Reports/Sum_winners _all.pdf

Neilans, T. & Isreal, A. (1981). Towards maintenance and generalization of behavior change: Teaching children self-regulation and self-instructional skills. *Cognitive Therapy and Research, 5,* 189-195.

Nelson, J. (1996). Designing schools to meet the needs of students who exhibit disruptive behavior. *Journal of Emotional and Behavioral Disorders, 4,* 147-161.

Nelson, J., Martella, R. & Garland, B. (1998). The effects of teaching school expectations and establishing consistent consequences on formal office disciplinary actions. *Journal of Emotional and Behavioral Disorders, 6,* 153-161.

Nelson, R., Roberts, M., Bullis, M., Albers, C. & Ohland, B. (2000). Functional behavior assessment: Looking beyond applied behavior analysis. In A. Canter (Ed.). *Behavioral interventions: Creating a safe environment in our schools* (pp.

25-27). Bethesda, MD: National Association of School Psychologists.

Nelson, D. & Quick, J. (2003). *Organizational behavior: Foundation realities and challenges.* U. S.: South-western.

Newsom, C., Favell, J. & Rincover, A. (1982). The side effects of punishment. In S. Axelrod and J. Apsche (Eds.), *The effects and side effects of punishment on human behavior.* New York: Academic Press.

N. Y. S. Office of Mental Retardation and Developmental Disabilities (OMRDD). (n.d.). *SCIP-R, Strategies for crisis intervention and prevention – Revised.* Albany, NY: Author.

Ollendick, T. & Madson, J. (1976). An initial investigation into the parameters of overcorrection. *Psychological Reports, 39,* 1139-1142.

Ollendick, T. & Madson, J. (1978). Overcorrection: An overview. *Behavior Therapy, 9,* 830-842.

O'Leary, K., Kaufman, K., Kass, R. & Drabman, R. (1970). The effects of loud and soft reprimands on the behavior of disruptive students. *Exceptional Children, 37,* 145-155.

O'Neil, R., Horner, R., Albin, R., Storey, K. & Sprague, J. (1997). *Functional assessment and program development for problem behaviors.* Pacific Grove, CA: Brooks/Cole.

O'Neil, R., Horner, R., Albin, R., Storey, K., Sprague, J. & Newton, J. (1997). *Functional assessment and program development for problem behavior: A practical handbook.* Pacific Grove, CA: Brooks/Cole.

Osher, D., Dwyer, K. & Jackson, S. (2004). *Safe, supportive and successful schools – Step by step.* Longmont, CO: Sopris West.

Patterson, D. & Basham, R. (n.d.). *Visualizing change: Spreadsheets and graphical representation across domains in human service practice.* Retrieved June 1, 2005, from http://www.uta.edu/ssw/basham/visualizying%20change.ppt

Payton, J., Wardlaw, D., Graczyk, P., Bloodworth, M., Tompsett, C. & Weissberg, R. (2000). Social and emotional learning: A framework for promoting mental health and reducing risk behavior in children and youth. *The Journal of School Health, 70* (5), 179-186.

Peterson, K. (1998). Establishing effective schoolwide behavior management and discipoine systems. Issue #10, Wisconsin Center for Education Research, School of Education, University of Wisconsin-Madison. Retrieved July 12, 2004, from http://www.wcer.wisc.edu

Peterson, G., Beekley, C., Speaker, K. & Pietrzak, D. (1996). An examination of violence in three rural school districts. *Rural Educator, 19* (3), 25-32.

Poland, S. & Pitcher, G. (1990). Best practices in crisis intervention. In A. Thomas and J. Grimes (Eds.), *Best practices in school psychology II.* Washington, D. C.: The National Association of School Psychologists.

Pray, J. (1999). *Excel 2000: Charting and organizing data.* Rochester, NY: Ziff-Davis Education.

Proctor, M. & Morgan, D. (1991). Effectiveness of a response-cost raffle procedure on the disruptive classroom behavior of adolescents with behavior problems. *School Psychology Review, 20,* 97-109.

Preator, K., Peterson, P., Jenson, W. & Ashcroft, P. (1984). Overcorrection and alternative response training in the reduction of an autistic child's inappropriate touching. *School Psychology Review, 13,* 107-110.

Professional Assault Response Training (PART) (2002). MTU Training Concepts, Pty Ltd.

Puckett, G. & Vogt, J. (1995). Use your computer to evaluate your programs. *Nonprofit World, 13* (1), 21-22.

Quinn, M., Osher, D., Hoffman, C. & Hanley, T. (1998). *Safe, drug-free and effective schools for ALL students: What works!* Washington, D.C.: U. S. Department of Education.

Quinn, M. & Rutherford, R. B. (1998). *Alternative programs for students with social, emotional or behavioral problems.* Reston, VA: Council for Children with Behavioral Disorders, a division of CEC.

Rathvon, N. (1999). *Effective school interventions: Strategies for enhancing academic achievement and social competence.* New York: The Guilford Press.

Salend, S. & Allen, E. (1985). Comparative effects of externally managed and self-managed response-cost systems on inappropriate classroom behavior. *Journal of School Psychology, 23,* 59-67.

Sattler, J. M. (2001). *Assessment of children: Behavioral and clinical applications, fourth edition.* New York: Jerome M. Sattler, Inc.

Schlichter, K. & Horan, J. (1981). Effects of stress inoculation on the anger and aggression management skills of institutionalized juvenile delinquents. *Cognitive Therapy and Research, 5* (4), 359-365.

Schmidt, J. (1997). *Making and keeping friends.* West Nyack, NY: The Center for Applied Research in Education.

Schwitzgebel, R. (1964). *Street corner research: An experimental approach to the juvenile delinquent.* Cambridge, MA: Harvard University Press.

Raywid, M. A. (1994). Alternative schools: The state of the art. *Educational Leadership, 52* (1), 26-31.

Residential Child Care Project, Family Life Development Center. (2002). *Therapeutic Crisis Intervention System Information Bulletin.* Cornell University: Author.

Rhode, G., Jensen, W. & Reavis, H. (1992). *The tough kid book: Practical classroom management strategies.* Longmont, CO: Sopris West.

Ringeisen, H., Henderson, K. & Hoagwood, K. (2003). Context matters: Schools and the "research to practice gap" in children's mental health. *School Psychology Review, 32* (2), 153-168.

Rintoul, B., Thorne, J., Wallace, I., Mobley, M., Goldman-Fraser, J. & Luckey, H. (1998). *Factors in child development: Personal characteristics and parental behavior – draft final report.* Centers for Disease Control and Prevention, U. S. Department of Health and Human Services. Research Triangle Park: NC.

Rossi, R. J. (1994). *Schools and students at risk: Context and framework for positive change.* New York: Teachers College Press.

Rossi, P. & Freeman, H. (1987). *Evaluation: A systematic approach.* Thousand Oaks, CA: Sage Publications.

Ryan, W. (1971). *Blaming the victim.* New York: Random House.

Scott, T. M. (2001). A school-wide example of positive behavioral support. *Journal of Positive Behavior Interventions, 3* (2), 88-95.

Shapiro, E. & Kratochwill, T. (Eds.). (2000). *Behavioral assessment in schools: Theory, research and clinical foundations.* New York: Guilford Press.

Sharpe, T. & Templin, T. (1997). Implementing collaborative teams: A strategy for school-based professionals. *Journal of Physical Education, Recreation and Dance, 68* (6), 50-56.

Sher, I. M. (1996). An analysis of the impact of school uniforms on students' academic performance and disciplinary behavior. *Dissertation Abstracts International: The Humanities & Social Sciences, 57*(1), 166-A.

Shores, R., Gunter, P. & Jack, S. (1993). Classroom management strategies: Are they setting events for coercion? *Behavioral Disorders, 18,* 92-102.

Skiba, R. J. (2000). Zero tolerance, zero evidence: An analysis of school disciplinary practice. *Indiana Education Policy Center, Policy Research Report # SRS2.*

Skiba, R. & Peterson, R. (1999). The dark side of zero tolerance. *Phi Delta Kappan, 80*, 372-376.

Skinner, B. F. (1953). *Science and human behavior.* New York: Free Press.

Sommerville, D. & McDonald, S. (2002). *Developing school and community partnerships to meet the needs of students with challenging behaviors.* Arlington, VA: The Council for Children with Behavioral Disorders and the Council of Administrators of Special Education, Divisions of the CEC.

Spivack, G. & Shure, M. (1974). *Social adjustment of young children: A cognitive approach to solving real-life problems.* San Francisco: Jossey-Bass.

Sprague, J., Sugai, G. & Walker, H. M. (1998). Antisocial behavior in schools. In T. S. Watson & F. M. Gresham (Eds.), *Handbook of child behavior therapy: Ecological considerations in assessment, treatment and evaluation.* New York: Plenum.

Sprick, R. & Howard, L. (1995). *The teachers' encyclopedia of behavior management: 100 problems / 500 plans.* Longmont, CO: Sopris West.

Sprick, R., Sprick, M. & Garrison, M. (1993). *Interventions: Collaborative planning for students at risk.* Longmont, CO: Sopris West.

Stanley, M. S. (1996). School uniforms and safety. *Education & Urban Society, 28*, 424-435.

Steinber, Z. (1992). Pandora's children. *Beyond Behavior*, spring edition, 5-13.

Stewart, J. (2002). *Beyond time out.* Gorham, ME: Hastings Clinical Associates.

Sudman, S. & Bradburn, N. (1982). *Asking questions: A practical guide to questionnaire design.* San Francisco: Jossey-Bass.

Sugai, G. & Horner, R. H. (1994). Including students with severe behavior problems in general education settings: Assumptions, challenges and solutions. In J. Marr, G. Sugai & G. Tindal (Eds.), *The Oregon Conference Monograph* (102-120). Eugene: University of Oregon.

Sugai, G. & Lewis, T. (1999). *Developing positive behavioral support for students with challenging behaviors.* Reston, VA: Council for Children with Behavioral disorders, a Division of CEC.

Thompon, R., Nelson, C., Spenceri, M. & Maybank, D. (1999). Safe and effective schools: The Boys Town model. *Caring, 15* (3), 10-15.

Thousand, J. & Villa, R. (1992). Collaborative teams: A powerful tool for school restructuring. In R. Villa, J. Thousand, W. Steinback & W. Stainback (Eds.), *Restructuring for caring and effective education*. Baltimore: Paul H. Brooks Publishing Company.

Tobin, T., Sugai, G. & Colvin, G. (1996). Patterns in middle school disciplinary records. *Journal of Emotional and Behavioral Disorders, 4* (2), 82-94.

Todd, A. Horner, R., Sugai, G. & Colvin, G. (1999). Individualizing school-wide discipline for students with chronic problem behaviors: A team approach. *Effective School Practices, 17,* 72-82.

U. S. General Accounting Office. (1993). GAO/PEMD – 10.1.7. *Developing and using questionnaires*. Washington, D.C.: Author.

VanHouten, R. (1982). Punishment: From the animal lab to the applied setting. In S. Axelrod & J. Apsche (Eds.), *The effects and side effects of punishment on human behavior*. New York: Academic Press.

Vygotsky, L. (1962). *Thought and language*. New York: Wiley.

Waldren, N. (1997). Inclusion. In G. Bear, K. Minke & A. Thomas (Eds.), *Children's needs II: Development, problems and alternatives*. Bethesda, MD: National Association of School Psychologists.

Walker, H. (1979). *The acting out child: Coping with classroom disruption*. Boston: Allyn & Bacon.

Ward, M. & Baker, B. (1968). Reinforcement therapy in the classroom. *Journal of Applied Behavior Analysis, 1,* 323-328.

Warger, C. (2001). *Research on full-service schools and students with disabilities*. Arlington, VA: ERIC Clearinghouse on Disabilities and Gifted Education.

Waxman, H., Wang, M., Anderson, K. & Walber, H. (1985). Adaptive education and student outcomes: A quantitative synthesis. *Journal of Educational Research, 78,* 228-236.

Wehlage, G. (1991). School reform for at-risk students. *Equity & Excellence in Education, 25* (1), 15-24.

Weist, M. D. (1999). Challenges and opportunities in expanded school mental health. *Clinical Psychology Review, 19,* 131-136.

Weist, M. & Christodulu, K. (2000). Expanded school mental health programs: Advancing reform and closing the gap between research and practice. *The Journal of School Health*, Kent: *70* (5), 195-201.

Weisz, J., Donenberg, G., Han, S., & Weiss, B. (1995). Bridging the gap between lab and clinic in child and adolescent psychotherapy. *Journal of Consulting and Clinical Psychology, 63,* 688-701.

West, J. F. (1990). Education collaboration in the restructuring of schools. *Journal of Educational and Psychological Consultation, 1* (1), 23-40.

West, J. F. & Idol, L. (1993). The counselor as consultant in the collaborative school. *Journal of Counseling & Development, 71* (6), 678-683.

White, A. & Barley, J. (1990). Reducing disruptive behaviors of elementary physical education students with sit and watch. *Journal of Applied Behavior Analysis, 23,* 353-359.

Whitman, T. & Johnston, M. (1983). Teaching addition and subtraction with regrouping to educable mentally retarded children: A group self-instructional training program. *Behavior Therapy, 14,* 127-143.

Wielkiewicz, R. M. (1986). *Behavior management in the schools: Principles and procedures.* New York: Pergamon Press.

Will, M. C. (1986). Educating children with learning problems: A shared responsibility. *Exceptional Children, 52,* 411-415.

Witt, J. & Elliott, S. (1982). The response-cost lottery: A time efficient and effective classroom intervention. *Journal of School Psychology, 20,* 155-161.

Woodruff, D., Osher, D., Hoffman, C., Gruner, A., King, M., Snow, S. & McIntire, J. (1999). The role of education in a system of care: Effectively serving children with emotional or behavioral disorders. In *Systems of care: Promising practices in children's mental health, 1998 Series, Vol. 111.* Washington, D.C.: Center for Effective Collaboration and Practice, American Institutes for Research, p. xiii.

Workman, E. (1982). *Teaching behavioral self-control to students.* Austin, TX: Pro-Ed.

Workman, E. & Hector, M. (1978). Behavior self-control in classroom settings: A review of the literature. *Journal of School Psychology, 16,* 227-236.

Wyka, G. & Gabriel, R. (1983). *National Crisis Prevention Institute Instructor's Manual.* Brookfield, WI: National Crisis Prevention Institute.

Ysseldyke, J. E. & Christenson, S. L. (1994). *The instructional environment system – II.* Longmont, CA: Sopris West.

Zins, J. E. , Curtis, M. J., Graden, J. L. & Ponti, C. R. (1988). *Helping students succeed in the regular classroom: A guide for developing intervention assistance programs.* San Francisco: Jossey-Bass.

LaVergne, TN USA
05 September 2010
195908LV00002B/32/A